The Fine Art of
JAPANESE
COOKING

HIDEO DEKURA

Bay Books
Sydney and London

Contents

About the Author

Hideo Dekura has been closely involved with Japanese food and cooking practically since the day he was born. His family operated a restaurant, Kihei of Tokyo, which his brother still runs.

From helping in the restaurant as a child he later progressed to cooking and giving demonstrations of the decorative Japanese arts including preparation and serving of Japanese food. His interest in cooking later led him to Europe to study classical French cooking. He is highly qualified in both western and Japanese cuisine.

Mr. Dekura came to Australia in 1972, having lived on the west coast of the USA for some years. He cooked in Japanese restaurants for several years before opening his own — the Japanese Garden at Chatswood. In 1974 he set up a Japanese catering company which initially served mainly Japanese business corporations with bases in Australia; the clientele has now greatly expanded, however, in the wake of the growing popularity of Japanese food.

Photography by Ashley Barber

Compiled and edited by Sue Doyle

Published by Bay Books
61–69 Anzac Parade,
Kensington NSW 2033

Publisher: George Barber

Copyright © 1984 Bay Books

National Library of Australia
Card number and ISBN 0 85835 768 2

Typesetting by Savage Type Pty Ltd

The publishers would like to thank Mrs. Anegawa of the Anegawa Trading Co., Kabuki Too restaurant and the Kabuki shop, Kambrook and Breville for loaned appliances and Voula Kyprianou for assistance with cooking and presentation.

Introduction

he preparation, serving and eating of Japanese food is much more than simply a means of satisfying hunger. It is an integral part of the fabric of Japanese culture, interwoven with aesthetics, tradition, religion and history. The two cardinal rules of the kitchen are that food must be very fresh and it must look beautiful when served. Japanese cuisine is uniquely refined, fastidious and subtle. Whereas western cooking tends to blend flavours, the Japanese prefer to retain the individual taste and appearance of each element in a dish. Each is relished separately for its own unique qualities. Food is served in small, meticulously prepared portions and fish plays a very important role. The Japanese have devised an amazing number of ways to prepare it.

The essence of Japanese cooking is its closeness to nature. Making the most of fresh, natural seasonal foods with the greatest possible culinary artistry is its keynote. When the strawberries arrive in February for example, they appear everywhere — in the best, most elegant restaurants and on the dinner tables of the humblest households. There are dozens of such foods — fruit, vegetables, fish, and eggs of various birds such as quail — which are forever linked, for the Japanese, with a particular season. Every food has its season and every season its food. The western preoccupation with exotic and out of season foods is regarded as quite peculiar.

To the uninitiated palate the tastes and textures of Japanese food may seem strange and even distasteful at first. Rest assured that many a reluctant sampler has become in time a devotee. One-pot meals such as sukiyaki and shabu shabu are probably the most easily accessible and satisfying to the westerner. Teriyaki (literally 'shining grill') dishes are also popular. But the subtler delights of a delectably fresh sashimi or a decorative tray of delicate sushi once experienced are never to be forgotten.

Traditional Japanese cooking, some feel, is in danger of a severe decline because of modern tastes for convenience foods. Western style restaurants and fast food chains flourish all over Japan. Ironically, Japanese food is fast gaining popularity in the west where Zen austerity has had a marked influence on cooking in recent years — the popularity of nouvelle cuisine and cuisine minceur bears witness to this. As well, general taste now tends more towards lighter, simpler meals and away from the richer dishes of classical cooking. People are more health conscious about their diets. They do not want to eat as much as in the past and are not as dependent on fats, dairy products and sugar.

To better understand the distinctive approach of the Japanese to food and eating it helps to know something of their history and culture.

History

The nature worship of the ancient Japanese laid the foundation for the national cuisine. This, and the fact that Japan has never produced crop surpluses because of its mountainous terrain, gave rise to two important elements in Japanese cooking — freshness and frugality. Contact with other peoples added other elements which the Japanese modified and made truly their own.

From the sixth through to the eighth centuries Japan had considerable contact with China, a more complex and sophisticated culture. The Chinese cultural influence was felt profoundly in all aspects of life including cuisine. Buddhism, with its deep respect for all forms of life and its prohibition of meat eating, was particularly influential. Tea and soybeans were both imported from China during this period.

Free contact with China came to an end in the middle of the ninth century with the collapse of the T'ang dynasty.

Then followed 400 years known as the Heian age, named for Japan's ancient capital of Heian-kyo (Kyoto). This was a golden age for Japanese culture when art and social life were perfected and refined to an amazing degree. An extremely elaborate code of etiquette developed governing just about every aspect of life from politics to lovemaking. Although food remained simple and natural, various complicated and decorative ways of presenting it were developed.

After the golden age came several centuries of war and civil strife and the rise to power of the samurai warriors. Savage and warlike though they undoubtedly were, the samurai did however favour ceremonial and elegant table etiquette. The fifteenth century saw the perfection of the Buddhist-inspired tea ceremony, the epitome of frugal refinement.

Toward the middle of the sixteenth century came the first contact with the western world via some adventurous Portuguese traders. Quite quickly, a flourishing trade relationship was established with Portugal. The Japanese regarded the foreigners as primitive barbarians, albeit shrewd and valuable trading partners. The Jesuit missionaries, led by St. Francis Xavier, who followed the merchants showed more sympathy with Japanese civilisation. Tempura, that most refined and light of deep-fried dishes, was actually adapted from traditional Portuguese deep fried food. Of course the Japanese characteristically refined the concept much further.

It was not until after the 1850s that Japan became very open to the influences of western industrialisation. The Japanese people found much to admire in dynamic capitalist civilisation and took to western ways with great enthusiasm and amazing success. They made particularly rapid progress in the field of science and technology and by the early twentieth century Japan was well on its way to becoming the industrial giant it is today. At the same time they borrowed western-style food and cooking and began to abandon the Buddhist vegetarian diet. Nowadays American fast food chains thrive throughout urban Japan although there is still great respect for traditional food. The practice of that most Japanese of customs, the tea ceremony, still enjoys enormous popularity and its intricate rules are carefully passed on from generation to generation.

The Tea Ceremony

Tea is Japan's national drink, taken with most meals and at practically any time of the day or night. But a uniquely complex set of rituals and customs known as the tea ceremony has come to be associated with drinking 'matcha', a special kind of powdered green tea. The tea ceremony is, however, much more than a formal social gathering — it has great aesthetic and spiritual significance which can be said to embody the very essence of the Japanese approach to life.

The historical roots of the tea ceremony reach back to the thirteenth century when Zen Buddhist monks used to drink tea ceremonially to aid them in their devotions. The rituals were elaborated and refined to an art form by the tea masters of the Imperial court of the fifteenth and sixteenth centuries. The many complicated rules laid down by the tea masters governed every aspect of the ceremony from the number of guests to the positioning of vessels and the size and proportions of the tea room. These rules are still observed today.

The vessels are arranged in a harmonious and artistic pattern. They are often objects of great beauty and antiquity in themselves. The host or hostess ritually cleans the teaspoon, tea caddy and tea bowl with a silk cloth called the 'fukusa'. The tea bowl is then washed with hot water from the traditional iron kettle which simmers over a charcoal fire. With great care and solemnity the green powdered tea is measured into the bowl with a special long bamboo teaspoon. Only the freshest, purest water is used to make the tea and it must be exactly the right temperature — very hot but not boiling or bubbling excessively. Finally the tea in the bowl is whisked with a 'chasen' or hand-made bamboo whisk, into a jade-coloured froth. The technique required to whip the tea just enough and with a vigorous yet graceful motion can take years to learn. The tea is drunk with formal, graceful movements and every nuance of flavour and aroma savoured fully. A simple tea ceremony takes about 40 minutes but if the traditional elegant meal or 'kaiseki' is served it can last for hours.

It is sometimes hard for westerners to understand the fastidious attention to detail so characteristic of the tea ceremony. Our practical, materialistic way of life leaves little room for such leisurely stateliness. For the Japanese however it is a valuable part of their social, cultural and spiritual heritage. Its formality and understated elegance can both refresh the senses and soothe the spirit.

Japan–Australia Relations

Japan is a vitally important country for Australia. Its cultural and economic impact on Australian society in the last 20 years has been enormous. During the 1960s and 1970s trade between the two countries expanded at an amazing rate and now Japan is one of Australia's foremost trading partners.

In recognition of this special relationship the Australia–Japan Foundation was established in 1976. The aims of the Foundation are to encourage a closer relationship between the Australian and Japanese peoples and to further their mutual knowledge and understanding. Encouraging people-to-people contact and promoting study and other activities is aimed at achieving these ends.

A Sister State Relationship between Tokyo and New South Wales was established in May 1984 to promote closer ties of friendship between the two states. Programs for mutual co-operation in trade, commerce, tourism, education, culture and sports are planned for the benefit of both regions. Various student exchange programs and the working holiday program for young people have also done much to help the Japanese and Australian people get to know each other.

There exists a mutual fascination between Japan and Australia which has resulted in a ready acceptance in both countries of seemingly exotic cultural influences. There has been a burgeoning of Japanese restaurants in Australia, partly in response to demand from Japanese expatriates but mostly to satisfy an enthusiastic local interest. Japanese food at its best can be sampled at many of these but hopefully it will also be produced more often in many Australian kitchens in the near future.

Japanese Restaurants

Sydney

Defune — 155–167 Miller Street North Sydney (02) 438 4895

Edosei — 74 Clarence Street Sydney 29 8746

Fuji Tempura Bar — 18 Ash Street Sydney 231 1740

Gohsyu Ramen Tei — 5 York Street Sydney

Hanaya — 42 Kellett Street Kings Cross 356 4222

Kabuki — 185A Bourke Street East Sydney 357 5050

Kabuki San — 373 Pitt Street Sydney 264 6668

Kabuki Too — 98 Bourke Street Woolloomooloo 358 2245

Kappa — 121 Walker Street North Sydney 922 4370

Kirakuya — 98 Falcon Street Crows Nest 929 3444

Kiyomasa (Mosman) — 3A Spit Road Mosman 969 1150

Kiyomasa (North Sydney) — 1 Napier Street North Sydney 922 5744

Komon — 114 Darlinghurst Road Darlinghurst 33 6803

Kyoto — Cremorne Plaza, 342 Military Road Cremorne 909 3865

Mikado — 178 Victoria Street Kings Cross 358 1873

Miyako — 459 New South Head Road Double Bay 327 2383

Nagoya Sukiyaki House — 186 Victoria Street Kings Cross 358 1873

Noriko — 10 Martin Place Sydney 232 5785

Shogun — 89 Macleay Street Potts Point 358 1778

Suehiro — 157 Walker Street North Sydney 922 5744

Suntory — 529 Kent Street Sydney 267 2900

Sushi House — 258 Pacific Highway Crows Nest 439 1494

Takenko — MG15 C.B.A. Centre, 273 George Street Sydney 27 4899

Tochigiya Robatayaki — 32 York Street Sydney 29 5799

Melbourne

Akasaka — 120 Exhibition Street Melbourne (03) 63 3129

Ibuki's — 26 Toorak Road South Yarra 26 4239

Kenzan — 45 Collins Street Melbourne 662 2933

Kuni's — 27 Crossley Street Melbourne 63 9243

Madame Butterfly — 76 Smith Street Collingwood 419 2397

Satsuma — 159 Spring Street Melbourne 662 2152

Shogun — Coverlid Place Melbourne 662 2471

Stone Garden (Sekitei) — 2F 169 Bourke Street Melbourne 63 7300

Sukiyaki House — 21 Alfred Place Melbourne 63 8420

Teppan-Yaki Inn — 145 Collins Street Melbourne 63 9431

Torimatsu — 571 Bourke Street Melbourne 61 3826

Yamato — 28 Corrs Lane Melbourne 663 1706

Gold Coast

Okoh — Equinox Building, Ocean Road Surfers Paradise (075) 38 8449

Brisbane

Sennari — 85 Elizabeth Street Brisbane (07) 231 4404

Shoki — 345 Queen Street Brisbane 229 6410

Adelaide

Fuji of Tokyo — 112 Hindley Street Adelaide (08) 51 2571

Kiku — 61 O'Connell Street North Adelaide 267 5417

Teppan-Yaki — 3 St. Anne's Place Parkside 272 1841

Hobart

Sakura — 85 Salamanca Place (002) 23 4773

Perth

Kyoto — 434 William Street Perth (09) 328 8084

Jun and Tommy — 117 Murray Street Perth 325 2606

Sukiyaki — 120 Grandstand Road Belmont 277 1147

Japanese Provisions

Sydney

Anegawa Trading Co.
16A Deepwater Road
Castle Cove
(02) 406 5452

Ichibankan Japanese Grocery
36 Nurses Walk   The Rocks
27 2667

Tokyo Mart
Shop 27 Northbridge Plaza,
Sailors Bay Road   Northbridge
95 6860

Sakura Shokai (Shoten)
100 Edinburgh Road   Castlecrag
95 1947

**Northbridge Fruit and
Vegetable Shop
(for Japanese vegetables)**
Northbridge Plaza   Northbridge

Melbourne

Japan Mart
568 Malvern Road   Prahran
(03) 51 9344

Miyajima Food Centre
2 Sanicki Crescent   Bentleigh
East
570 3321

Tokyo Mart
584 Glenhuntly Road
Elsternwick
523 6200

Suzuran
159 Union Road
Surrey Hills
890 3950

Brisbane

Ocean Trading Co.
Cnr. Kessels Road and Logan Road
Mt. Gravatt
(07) 343 4451

Nikko International
Queens Arcade, 77 Queen Street
Brisbane
229 3069

Adelaide

Asian Kitchen
34 Gouger Street   Adelaide
(08) 51 2021

**Athens Continental Food
Market**
3 Western Mall   Central Market
51 2260

Boomerang Supermarket
161 The Parade   Norwood
31 6056

Hobart

Sakura
85 Salamanca Place   Hobart
(002) 23 4773

Bellerive Chinese Emporium
29 Cambridge Road   Bellerive
44 4625

Prasad Wholefoods
249 Sandy Bay Road   Sandy Bay
23 7540

Perth

Japanese Food Centre
113 Murray Street   Perth
(09) 325 3929

Japanese groceries. Anegawa Trading Co., Sydney

Techniques
Filleting snapper

   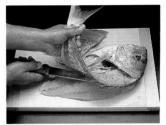

1. Thoroughly scale fish.

2. Holding the fish firmly on the board with your left hand cut into the back below the head with the point of the knife and continue to cut downwards, working as close as possible to the skeleton.

3. Repeat this process along the belly and gently lift off the whole fillet.

4. Hold the tail in your left hand and cut upwards towards the head, keeping knife just below the skeleton.

Vegetable cutting

Carrot

1. Peel the carrots.

2. Cut each carrot in half vertically and then into thin slices.

3. Cut each piece lengthwise into even-sized sticks.

4. Cut sticks into tiny dice.

Daikon

1. Wash and peel daikon.

2. Cut in half lengthwise and slice into half rounds *or*

3. Grate into needle shreds.

Onion

1. Peel onion and cut in half lengthwise.

2. Slice finely but do not cut through completely.

3. Chop into fine dice.

Cabbage

1. Peel off coarse outer leaves.

2. Slice in half lengthwise.

3. Chop into fairly large pieces.

Turnip

1. Peel and trim turnip.

2. Slice into very thin rounds with a sharp vegetable knife.

3. Cut rounds into 4 pieces.

Shallot

1. Trim shallots and peel away coarse outer leaves.

2. Slice very thinly into diagonal pieces *or*

3. Chop into fine rounds.

Cucumber

1. Peel one thin slice of peel from each side of cucumber with a vegetable peeler.

2. Halve cucumber and scoop out seeds.

3. Slice very thinly.

Presentation garnishes

Western visitors to Japanese restaurants are often entranced by the chef's deft and delicate wielding of the vegetable knife — done in full view of diners — to produce decoratively cut and shaped vegetables for presentation garnishes. Quaint and beautiful flowers, leaves, animals and geometric or lace-like patterns adorn platters of sushi and sashimi or clear bowls of soup or dipping sauce.

Although it can take years to master traditional cutting techniques, some garnishes are quite simple to make and it is rewarding to try a few of them for yourself. They make a spectacular presentation and add an aesthetic dimension to cooking not much emphasised in western cuisine.

Method of cutting and shape varies with the vegetables you have to work with and are designed to make the most of flavour as well as colour and texture. Cylindrical vegetables such as carrot and daikon lend themselves to thin circular or half-moon sections, lotus root to complex lacy patterns and cucumber peel to ribbon-like garnishes. The firm texture of carrot and daikon make them very versatile for garnishes.

1. Carrot, zucchini, daikon and spray of pine needles, mushroom.

2. Pumpkin and cucumber skin.

3. Baby squash, lotus root, shallot, red radish.

4. Red radish with ginkgo nut, lemon, cucumber, carrot.

5. Cucumber, shredded daikon, daikon leaves, turnip.

6. Carrot, cucumber, leek, carrot.

7. Lemon, carrot, cucumber and lemon peel, cucumber, carrot.

8. Camellia leaves and green ginger, cucumber peel, cucumber, carrot.

Vegetable sculpture

This type of vegetable sculpture is called Muki-mono. The muki-mono technique can be used with many different vegetables. The vegetables are sometimes carved to resemble Japanese Ike-Bana flower arrangements. A lot of skill and patience is essential to obtain a perfect sculpture.

Ice carving is another decorative technique used in Japanese cuisine.

1. Use a sharp knife to cut the stem off the pumpkin and carefully remove all the seeds.

2. With a sharp tool begin carving approximately 5 cm from the top of the pumpkin. Carve away the skin so the top of the pumpkin resembles the neck and lip of a vase.

3. Use a black felt-tipped pen to write the message on the flesh of the pumpkin and carve the skin away from that area. The message written on this one is 'Beautiful Japan'.

4. Continue to carve away the skin to make the lettering stand out.

Utensils and implements

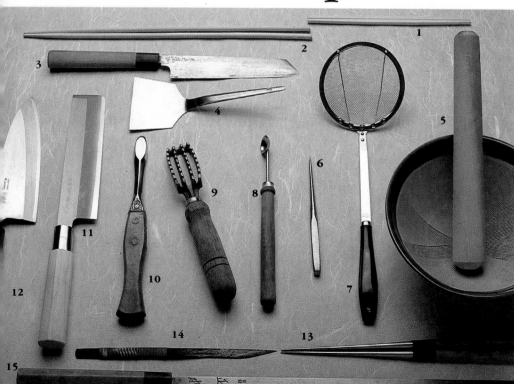

1. Disposable chopsticks
2. Bamboo cooking chopsticks
3. Muki-mono knife
4. Scraper (for pancakes and teppan-yaki)
5. Mortar and pestle
6. Skewer for securing eel to chopping board
7. Strainer (for fried food)
8. Scoop for fruit or vegetables
9. Fish scaler
10. Opener for shellfish
11. Vegetable cleaver
12. Fish knife
13. Steel chopsticks (for sashimi arrangement)
14. Vegetable carving/chiselling knife
15. Sashimi knife

Japanese chopsticks

Traditionally all Japanese food except soup is eaten with chopsticks and chopsticks are used to cook with as well.

Japanese chopsticks have pointed ends, unlike the Chinese variety which have blunt ends. They are well suited to Japanese cuisine; extreme care is taken with food presentation and the pointed ends can be used to carefully pick up each piece of food, keeping the arrangement on the platter looking beautiful throughout the meal.

For the Japanese people chopsticks serve as knife, fork and spoon at the table. For everyday meals, short, rounded lacquered chopsticks are used. Formal meals call for special cedarwood chopsticks and on very casual occasions short, flat, wooden disposable chopsticks with blunt ends may be used. Disposable chopsticks are inexpensive and convenient to use and may be purchased in many oriental stores.

Kitchen chopsticks are 2 to 3 times longer than ordinary eating chopsticks. They allow one-handed manipulation of all kinds of food and are useful for all types of Japanese cooking, be it deep-frying, pot-cooking, sushi making, pickling or the making of desserts.

When setting the table for a Japanese meal, chopsticks are never laid flat on the table. They rest on special chopstick rests or holders made of porcelain, pottery or bamboo. The chopsticks are placed in front of the guest side by side with both points resting on the holder and facing to the left. Chopsticks facing to the right mean bad luck to the Japanese. Between courses the chopsticks are always placed on the rests. It is considered ill-mannered to place them on the plate or in the bowl.

To use chopsticks:

○ Place one chopstick onto the crook of the thumb approximately one third of the way down the thicker end of the stick.

○ The chopstick should rest on the inside tip of the ring finger.

○ Place the second chopstick between the index and middle fingers (as you would hold a pencil), and press it against these fingers with the cushion of the thumb. (The point of the top chopstick should be kept extended slightly past the point of the chopstick below.)

○ Keeping the lower stick motionless, slide the upper stick down to meet the lower one and gently pick up the pieces of food by bending the index and middle fingers.

○ Do not hold the chopsticks too close to the point as control or leverage is lost and it becomes quite difficult to pick up food.

○ Do not hold chopsticks tightly in the hand or they will be difficult to manipulate. They should be held comfortably in the hand, allowing flexibility to open and close them.

○ When setting the table, lay the chopsticks in front of the guest on a rest, with the points facing to the left.

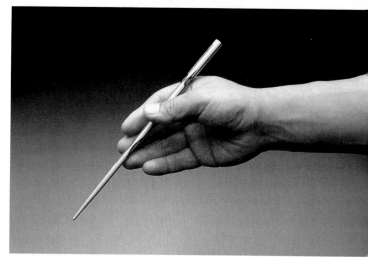

1. Hold one chopstick in crook of thumb, resting on inside tip of ring finger.

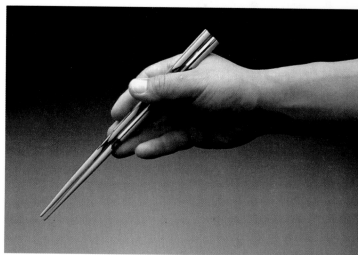

2. Place second chopstick in a similar position then press it between index and middle fingers with ball of thumb.

3. Bend index and middle fingers and slide upper stick down to meet lower one to pick up food.

12

Sushi

Sushi is extremely popular both with westerners and with the Japanese people themselves. Indeed there are more sushi restaurants in Japan than any other kind. It is true for many people that once tasted they quickly become a passion. The natural taste of fresh raw fish and shellfish is a perfect complement to the delicately vinegared rice on which it is served.

There are a number of varieties of sushi using different ingredients and prepared in different ways. But all varieties include the vinegared sushi rice, all are served in bite-sized pieces and all are presented with great care and artistry.

Nigiri-zushi — a core of moulded rice with topping, usually seafood

Nori-maki — rice and other ingredients rolled up in nori seaweed and cut into rounds

Tamago-yaki — omelette, either thick or thin, used as a base or covering for sushi

Inari-zushi — bean curd pouches stuffed with mixed, vinegared rice.

Combination sushi platter

How to eat sushi

The preferred ways to eat sushi are with chopsticks or with the fingers. To eat with the fingers:

1. With thumb, index and middle fingers simply pick up a piece of nigiri-zushi and turn it over.

2. Dip only the topping (not the rice) in soy sauce.

3. Slide the sushi into your mouth with the topping facing downwards so it comes into immediate contact with the taste buds.

4. Only a small amount of soy sauce should accompany sushi, to complement not camouflage its delicate flavour.

Sushi is generally accompanied by paper-thin slices of vinegar-pickled ginger. Eat small slices of ginger between servings of sushi to cleanse the palate, or place a thin slice of ginger on top of the sushi before eating.

Sushi rice

There are two main types of rice grown throughout the world — the Japanese variety (Japonica) and the Indian variety (Indica). Japanese-style rice has short, round grains and is sticky when cooked. Indian-style rice has long, narrow grains that, even when cooked, remain loose and separate. Long grain rice is good sauced with oriental foods but does not lend itself to sushi because of its dryness.

Rice that is still firm and resilient when steamed is preferred for nigiri-zushi and rolled sushi. A softer steamed rice is better for moulded sushi.

To prepare sushi rice

To make good sushi, the rice must be cooked in the right way, with care and understanding.

Rice
3⅓ cups short-grain rice
4 cups water

Vinegar mixture
5 tablespoons plus 1 teaspoon rice vinegar
5 tablespoons sugar
4 teaspoons salt

Wash rice until water runs clear and drain in a fine strainer for 1 hour. Put the drained rice in a rice cooker or a pot with a tight-fitting lid and add water. Cover and bring to boil over medium heat. Cover tightly and boil over high heat for 2 minutes. Reduce heat and boil for a further 5 minutes. Cook gently over a low heat for 15 minutes, or until all the water has been absorbed. Remove from heat. Take off lid, spread a clean kitchen towel over the top of pot, replace lid and let stand for 15 minutes. While rice is cooking, combine the vinegar mixture ingredients in a bowl and heat gently till the sugar has dissolved, stirring constantly. Remove from heat. To cool quickly, place in a bowl of ice cubes.

Empty rice into a hangiri (or other non metallic tub) and spread evenly over the base with a large wooden spoon. Run the spatula through the rice in right-and-left slicing motion to separate the grains. As you do this, slowly add the vinegar mixture. You may not need it all. The rice must not be mushy.

Continue the slicing motion with the spatula as you add the vinegar. Have a helper fan the rice with a fan (uchiwa) or a large piece of cardboard until the rice reaches room temperature. The fanning and mixing takes about 8 minutes. Do not refrigerate the rice, but keep it in the tub covered with a clean cloth until ready for use. Sushi rice lasts only one day and does not lend itself to the usual ways of dealing with leftovers.

1. Ingredients: rice, rice vinegar, mirin, sugar, salt.

2. Pour vinegar mixture into rice in hangiri.

3. Run spoon or spatula through rice to separate grains.

4. Prepared sushi rice.

To prepare sushi prawns

Prawns to be used as sushi topping must be well coloured and shaped and carefully opened out to encase the fine finger of sushi rice underneath. Simply prepare and chill until required.

1. Before poaching, slide a bamboo skewer under the shell just above the legs of each prawn to prevent it curling. The skewer should not touch the flesh.
2. Poach lightly in salted water, until the flesh changes colour. Remove from water, drain and slide skewer from the prawn.

3. Remove the head and shell leaving the tail attached. Trim the small pieces of shell from above the tail. This requires patience and a very sharp knife.
4. Carefully make an incision along the underside of the prawn.
5. Deepen the incision so that the prawn can be opened and flattened. Do not cut all the way through as the prawn will fall apart. Devein the prawn.
6. Lightly press the prawn flat to prepare it for use as a topping.

Temaki-zushi (Californian roll)

As its name implies, this is a very new, modern type of Japanese maki-zushi. The ingredients and method are the same as for traditional maki-zushi except that the hands are used for rolling instead of a bamboo mat. Maki-zushi consists of vinegared rice, vegetables and fish tightly rolled in seaweed with the aid of a bamboo mat. Temaki-zushi however should not be tightly rolled. By using the hands the filling remains loose.

2 sheets dried seaweed
1 avocado
1 tin salmon caviar
1 small cucumber
1 teaspoon wasabi (green mustard)
1 teaspoon toasted sesame seeds
1 cup sushi rice

Cut the seaweed in half. Peel the avocado and cut into small pieces. Peel, cut and seed the cucumber; slice thinly and set aside.

Spread a piece of seaweed with ¼ cup rice. Sprinkle ¼ teaspoon toasted sesame seeds over the rice. Place 2 slices of cucumber over the sesame seeds. Divide the caviar into 4 and spread one portion over the cucumber. Finally place some of the avocado over the caviar and using both hands roll up loosely. Repeat method until all ingredients are used. Each temaki-zushi should be about 10 cm long.

Temaki-zushi is currently enjoying a world wide vogue. It is especially popular in America and is becoming equally so in Australia. Its popularity is due to the fact that the ingredients are readily available on the western market and it is quite simple to prepare. Temaki-zushi is a good dish to serve when entertaining.
Serves 4

Tekka-maki (Tuna roll)

5 half sheets dried seaweed
3 cups sushi rice
1 tablespoon wasabi
thinly sliced fresh tuna

Spread a layer of rice over one piece of seaweed. Spread a small amount of wasabi evenly over the rice and place some thinly sliced tuna on top.

Gently but firmly roll the seaweed up to form a long, thin cylinder. Using a sharp knife cut along the cylinder to form rounds approximately 2.5 cm wide. Arrange on a dish and serve.
Serves 4

Suzume-zushi (Baby snapper)

1 baby snapper (about 10 cm long)
1 cup white vinegar
2 tablespoons sugar
pinch salt
½ cup dashi (see stocks chapter)
¼ cup mirin wine

Combine vinegar, sugar, salt, dashi and mirin wine together and set aside.

Clean and scale baby snapper. Remove head, leaving fins and tail intact.

Run knife down spine of the fish and open out butterfly style. Remove backbone.

Sprinkle snapper with salt and allow to stand 10 minutes, then wash salt off the fish, and place in the marinade for half an hour. Use for nigiri-zushi.
Serves 2
Note: Salting prior to marinating fish in vinegar in Japan is called shimeru.

Kobana-maki *(Rolled omelette)*

2 thin Japanese omelettes
  (p.69)
2 pieces dried seaweed
1 cup sushi rice
100 g pickled ginger
½ cucumber
1 × 7.5 cm piece pickled
  horseradish
⅛ teaspoon wasabi
  (Japanese mustard)

Make omelettes and allow to cool. Place one sheet of dried seaweed onto a bamboo mat. Take one omelette and lay over the seaweed. Divide the sushi rice into 2 portions and spread one portion over the omelette. Gently press down onto the rice with hands to flatten slightly. Peel and thinly slice the cucumber into long strips and divide these into 2 portions. Slice the pickled horseradish into long thin strips and divide into 2 portions. Place half the strips of cucumber and horseradish over the rice as the final layer. Spread a tiny amount of wasabi over the vegetables.

Using both hands and pressing firmly, bring the bamboo mat up from underneath and roll to form a long cylinder. Remove the mat and using a sharp knife cut the roll into 5 cm lengths.

Follow the same procedure for the remaining ingredients. Arrange on a plate and serve.
Serves 4

Hadaka-maki *(Unclad seaweed roll)*

1 cup sushi rice
1 cucumber
1 square omelette
2 pieces dried seaweed
1 teaspoon toasted sesame
  seeds
⅛ teaspoon wasabi (green
  mustard)

Cut a sheet of plastic wrap and use it to cover a chopping board. Place sushi rice on the plastic wrap and flatten, pressing firmly. Layer both sheets of seaweed over the rice. Spread wasabi over the seaweed. Slice the cucumber thinly and place 2 slices across the length of the seaweed. Place the omelette on top as the final layer.

Gently lift the plastic wrap from the board and roll the ingredients up firmly using the hands. Use a bamboo mat (sudare) outside the plastic as an aid to shaping the hadaka-maki into a rectangle.

Carefully remove the mat and plastic from the roll and using a sharp knife cut into 2.5 cm lengths. Arrange on a dish and serve.
Serves 4

Anago *(Sea eel Tokyo style)*

1 sea eel (about 30 cm long)
1 cup water
½ cup sugar
1½ tablespoons mirin wine
½ cup soy sauce

Clean the eel and remove head and bones but do not discard. Fillet eel from the back and open out butterfly style.

In a saucepan combine the water, sugar, mirin wine and soy sauce. Add eel head and bones and heat over a moderate flame to make a stock.

When mixture is hot, add filleted eel and cook on low heat for half an hour.

Remove fillets and continue to heat anago sauce (containing the head and bones), over medium heat until thick. Strain. This sauce is called nitsume and can be used whenever a fish stock is required.

The anago fish is formed into rectangles with sushi rice the same way as nigiri-zushi. The nitsume is brushed over the moulded anago prior to serving.
Serves 4
Note: As a serving suggestion, 50 g of rock sugar may be added to the anago sauce during the thickening stage to enhance the flavour.

Morikomi-zushi

Morikomi-zushi is a combination of sushi arranged and served in one large container. Nigiri-zushi, maki-zushi and even oshi-zushi are all suitable for presentation in this way. An arrangement of morikomi-zushi looks very attractive and is convenient to eat, making it an ideal party dish.

Saiku-zushi *(Fancy fish)*

½ cup sushi rice
1 sheet dried seaweed
skin of half cucumber
30 g caviar
1 small cuttlefish

Form sushi rice into 5 balls and flatten with the fingers to a diameter of 4.5 cm. Carefully wrap the seaweed around each ball of sushi rice.

Using a sharp knife cut skin of the cucumber into 5 garnishes, one for each ball. Arrange the 5 balls on a serving dish and place a cucumber garnish on each one.

Clean and skin the cuttlefish (see p.24). Cut flesh into small squares and place one square as a garnish on each rice ball. Using a teaspoon, place a small portion of caviar on the top of each cuttlefish square and serve.
Serves 2

Camellia-zushi

½ cup sushi rice
100 g sashimi tuna fish
1 hard-boiled egg yolk
camellia leaves for garnish

Using both hands mould sushi rice into a ball. Cut the tuna into 4 thin slices, sashimi style.

Using one slice of fish at a time, press onto the ball of sushi rice and shape to resemble the petals of the camellia flower. Continue to do so until all four slices of tuna are used. (The top of the rice ball should be visible and not covered by the fish.)

Pass the egg yolk through a strainer to produce fine threads of yolk. Carefully sprinkle the yolk over the centre of your 'flower' to represent the pollen.

Arrange camellia leaves or any similar green garnish around the base of the flower and serve.
Note: When catering for large groups allow one 'camellia' per person.

Yoshoku-zushi *(Western-style sushi)*

Yoshoku-zushi is made using ingredients familiar to the people of the western world. All the sushi family can be called yoshoku-zushi when western ingredients are substituted for Japanese. Some ingredients for yoshoku-zushi are smoked ham, roast beef, raw meat, salami, frankfurts, cheese, canned anchovies and olives.

The popularity of yoshoku-zushi is mainly due to the fact that many traditional Japanese ingredients are not easily obtainable.

Oshi-zushi/Battera-zushi

Oshi-zushi is made using a special oshi-zushi container which is simply a frame with a lid but no base, usually square.

1 quantity sushi rice
1 × 25 cm slimy mackerel
1 large piece dried kelp
1 cup white vinegar
2 tablespoons sugar
pinch salt
½ cup dashi (see stock chapter)
¼ cup mirin wine

Combine vinegar, sugar, salt, dashi and mirin wine and use to marinate the dried kelp and slimy mackerel which is treated the same way as the baby snapper in suzume-zushi (see p. 15).

Half fill the oshi-zushi container with rice. Layer the marinated kelp over the rice to completely cover. Place another layer of sushi rice on top of the kelp.

Arrange the sliced mackerel over the rice. Using the lid from the oshi-zushi container, press firmly down onto the mackerel.

To make battera-zushi correctly, an oshi-zushi container is essential. It is also essential that slimy mackerel be used.

Lift off the lid and remove the frame. You will have a square piece of battera-zushi.

Using a sharp knife cut the battera-zushi into 5 cm squares and serve.
Serves 2–4

Nigiri-zushi

Nigiri-zushi are raw fish topped sushi with a core of moulded rice. Nigiri means 'squeezed' in Japanese.

Using a sharp knife, cut the flesh of a suitable fish, e.g. salmon, into thin slices. Using the index finger place a little mustard onto the slices.

Hold a slice of fish in the left hand and mould the rice into a ball with the right hand. Place the rice ball into your left hand onto the slice of fish.

Using both hands mould the fish around the rice gently. Flatten slightly and form into a rectangular shape.

Using two fingers, make an indentation across the top of the rectangle, flattening it slightly.

The sushi should be 5 cm long.
Note: Remember that the size of the slice of fish must always be larger than the ball of rice when moulding nigiri-zushi into shape.

1. Cut flesh into long, thick pieces.

2. Using a fish knife slice pieces very thinly on a slight angle.

3. Place rice ball onto a slice of fish.

4. Gently mould fish around rice.

Chirashi-zushi

Chirashi-zushi

Chirashi-zushi requires the use of a variety of sushi sliced fish, as well as Japanese vegetables from the hills.

The beautifully sliced fish for this dish is arranged over a bed of sushi rice sprinkled with toasted sesame seeds.

A selection of vegetables is usually arranged with the fish.

Chakin-zushi *(Silk square sushi)*

5 thin Japanese omelettes
2 cups sushi rice
50 g pickled ginger (gari)
½ thinly sliced cucumber
1 teaspoon toasted sesame seeds
2 Japanese mushrooms, chopped

1 tablespoon green peas
100 g cooked, shelled prawns
5 thin, long strips cucumber peel

Combine sushi rice, pickled ginger, cucumber, sesame seeds, Japanese mushrooms, green peas and prawns in a bowl.

Divide the sushi rice mixture into five. Place one portion of the rice into the centre of an omelette and bring the side up and around the filling to form a pouch. Tie the ends with cucumber peel.

Repeat the process until all 5 chakin-zushi are completed.
Serves 5

Kappa-maki *(Cucumber roll)*

5 half sheets dried seaweed
3 cups sushi rice
1 tablespoon wasabi (green mustard)
½ cucumber, thinly sliced

Spread a layer of rice over one piece of seaweed. Spread a small amount of wasabi evenly over the rice and place some sliced cucumber on top.

Using a bamboo mat gently but firmly roll the seaweed up to form a long, thin cylinder.

Using a sharp knife cut along the cylinder at regular intervals to form rounds approximately 2.5 cm wide.

Arrange the kappa-maki on a dish to serve.
Serves 4–6

1. Spread a layer of rice over seaweed on bamboo mat.

2. Place cucumber on rice spread with wasabi.

3. Roll up bamboo mat.

4. Cut into 2.5 cm rounds.

Futo-maki *(Rolled omelette)*

This recipe is similar to kobana-maki except that the size and shape differ — futo-maki are larger rounds. This is a Tokyo style recipe. In the Osaka style, spinach leaves and vegetables from the hills are added to the filling before it is rolled up, and the sushi rice is sweetened.

2 sheets dried seaweed
3 cups sushi rice
½ cucumber
50 g pickled ginger
2 small, thin Japanese omelettes
1 tablespoon sesame seeds
1 tablespoon wasabi (green mustard)
2 pieces horseradish pickle (takuan)

Combine the rice, cucumber and ginger. Place a bamboo mat on flat surface and put one slice of seaweed on mat. Layer one omelette over the seaweed and place half the rice on top. Spread half the wasabi over the rice and sprinkle with half the toasted sesame seeds. Finally place one piece of horseradish pickle on top of the sesame seeds.

Using both hands, gently roll the bamboo mat to form a fat cylinder. Using a sharp knife cut into large rounds. Repeat the process using remaining ingredients.

Arrange futo-maki on a plate and serve.
Serves 2–4

Inari-zushi *(Sukeroku)*

Traditionally sukeroku means inari-zushi + nori-maki (seaweed rolls).

5 inari (bean curd bags), pre-cooked
1 cup sushi rice
2 tablespoons toasted sesame seeds

Cut each inari in half. Open the halved inari to form a pocket and place a ball of sushi rice inside. Sprinkle the rice with toasted sesame seeds and press the inari openings closed with the fingers. Repeat this process until all the inari are used.

To serve inari-zushi, place on a plate, cut side down. To make them look more interesting, they may be tied with thin strips of cucumber skin or kampyo (stalks from dried morning glory flowers).

The ends of the inari bags may also be tucked underneath to neaten their appearance.

Inari can be purchased cooked or uncooked. Here is a suggestion for preparation of uncooked inari.

½ cup soy sauce
1 ½ tablespoons mirin wine
½ cup sugar
¼ cup water or dashi (see stocks chapter)

Combine ingredients and place over a low heat. Immerse inari in the hot liquid and cook on low for 30 minutes. Remove inari from liquid and drain. Allow to cool then use as instructed above.
Serves 5

Sashimi

Sliced Raw Seafood

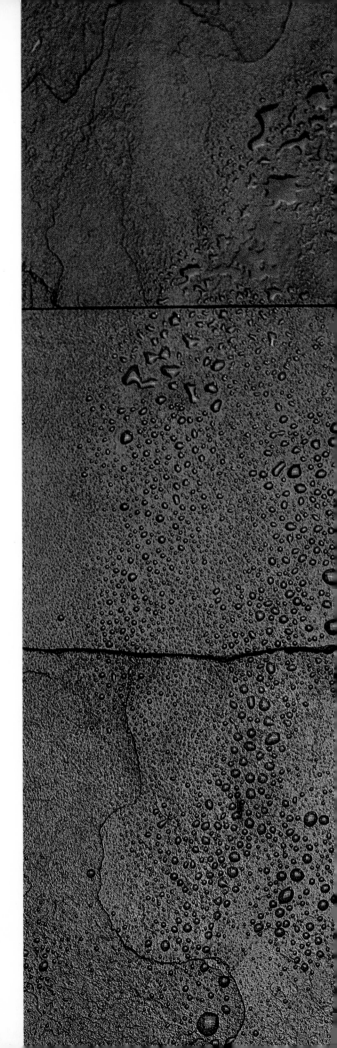

Sashimi is in many ways the very soul of Japanese cuisine. It is served at every formal meal — always early so that the palate has not been dulled by the more obvious flavour of cooked food — and displays the skill of the chef in choosing the best and freshest fish and in knifework and presentation.

Great care is exercised in the preparation of sashimi at every stage. The most crucial step is choosing the fish. It cannot be emphasised too much that it must be the very freshest available. Frozen seafood is definitely not suitable for sashimi. In Japan the fish is often killed and bled just before being cut and served as sashimi. Some of the recipes in this chapter call for live fish but this may not always be practical. The Sydney Fish Markets now stock many of the fish suitable for sashimi such as tuna and jewfish and will sell pieces of the flesh suitable for sashimi style cutting. Buy from a reputable fishmonger and test for freshness. Look for bright, prominent eyes, bright red gills, firm, elastic flesh and a fresh, pleasant smell.

Presentation is also extremely important. A finished platter of sashimi should look as delicate and beautiful as it tastes. Accompanying dipping sauces should be light, tangy and freshly made. Thicker cuts of sashimi can stand stronger flavoured sauces than very thin ones.

Fine, lean beef, either chopped or thinly sliced, can also be served raw, sashimi style.

Odori (dancing green prawns)

Ika *(Cuttlefish)*

3 cuttlefish (sumi-ika)
½ sheet dried seaweed
¼ teaspoon wasabi
1 × 7.5 cm piece shallot
    stalk
1 tablespoon pickled ginger
¼ cup grated horseradish
fresh basil seeds

Clean and skin the cuttlefish following sashimi instructions. Using a sharp knife, hold the cuttlefish flat on a board and carefully run the knife through it leaving a join at the end. Open out to give 2 thin fillets, butterfly style, about the same size.

Lay the seaweed over one half of the opened out cuttlefish. Place wasabi, shallot stalk and pickled ginger over the seaweed. Fold over other half of cuttlefish to cover.

Carefully roll cuttlefish into a cylinder and cut into 1 cm rounds. Arrange cuttlefish

rounds on a plate and serve garnished with horseradish and some fresh basil seeds.
Serves 2–3

1. Remove hard beak.

2. Take out innards.

3. Peel skin away from flesh.

Ika-no-sashimi (cuttlefish)

Koi-no-arai *(Crispy carp in iced water)*

2 live carp

In Japan live jewfish is more commonly used than carp (see following recipe). The fish is cut at the back of the head so the blood escapes, leaving the flesh clean and crisp.

Clean and fillet the carp.

Slice the fillets thinly, sashimi style, and plunge immediately into ice cold water for 5 minutes. This will shrink and crisp the flesh.

Remove fish from the water and arrange on a serving plate. Serve accompanied by soy sauce, wasabi and lemon slices.

Serves 2

Note: The fish must be eaten immediately it is removed from the iced water.

Suzuki-no-arai *(Crispy jewfish in iced water)*

1 small, live jewfish

Suzuki-no-arai is prepared using a live jewfish, cut at the back of the head and bled as in the preceding recipe.

Clean and fillet the jewfish. Immediately after the fish is filleted it should be sliced thinly, sashimi style. Then plunge quickly into ice cold water for 5 minutes to shrink and crisp the flesh.

Serve and eat as soon as possible accompanied by soy sauce, wasabi and lemon wedges.

Serves 2–3

Note: This method of preparation is similar to for dancing prawns.

Odori *(Dancing green prawns)*

5 live green tiger prawns
400 g ice cubes *or* party ice
½ lemon, sliced
1 small carrot, shredded
100 g shredded daikon
5 thinly sliced cucumber rounds
1 dessertspoon wasabi

Seaweed roll
1 large green tiger prawn
1 sheet dried seaweed

Cut heads and tails off the 5 prawns and set aside. Remove shells and chop flesh into 1.25 cm pieces. Mix flesh into the ice and allow to stand for 5 minutes.

To make the seaweed roll, peel single prawn completely and chop flesh. Spread prawn flesh over the sheet of dried seaweed and roll up tightly. Cut into 2.5 cm lengths.

Arrange the head and tail of each prawn on an individual serving plate. Place a portion of the iced flesh alongside the head and garnish with lemon slices, seaweed rolls, shredded carrot and daikon, sliced cucumber and wasabi. Soy sauce may be served separately in a small shallow bowl.

Serves 4

1. Shell prawns and remove heads and tails.

2. Slice down back

3. Cut flesh into 1.25 cm pieces.

Tako *(Octopus)*

1 medium-sized local octopus
2 litres water
½ cup salt
¼ cup vinegar
1 tablespoon salt
50 g fresh, tender seaweed, shredded

Rub whole octopus with the salt to remove all sliminess. Place water and vinegar in saucepan and bring to the boil.

Holding octopus by its tentacles gently dip it in and out of the water three times. This will stabilise the skin colour and prevent skin from splitting. Then carefully place the octopus in the water and cook for 4 minutes on high heat, turning occasionally.

Continue to cook a further 3 minutes on medium heat.

Remove from hot liquid and plunge into icy cold water, so it shrinks and cools at the same time. Remove from cold water, turn the head inside out and remove all the guts. Clean head thoroughly and turn right side out.

To serve, the octopus can be diced or thinly sliced sashimi style or marinated in sweet and sour vinegar (sunomono) beforehand. Serve on a bed of shredded seaweed.

Serves 4

Isebi-no-ikezukuri *(Live green lobster)*

1 medium-sized live green
  lobster
100 g fresh tuna, sliced
  sashimi style
1 sheet dried seaweed
1 small cucumber
100 g horseradish, sliced
½ tablespoon wasabi (green
  mustard)
2 cups ice cubes or party ice
soy sauce

Insert a sharp knife through the lobster flesh where the tail meets the head. Carefully separate the head and tail from the lobster. Remove brain and serve separately. Gently remove lobster meat from the tail shell and head and chop into 2.5 cm pieces.

Place lobster pieces into a bowl and mix in the ice. Allow to stand for 5 minutes to make the flesh crisp.

Remove flesh from the ice and replace in shell. Arrange lobster on a bed of shredded horseradish on a long serving platter. Slice cucumber into thin strips and arrange to cover the seaweed. Layer the tuna over cucumber and roll up tightly to form a long cylinder. Cut into 2.5 cm pieces. Serve the lobster garnished with the seaweed rolls, lemon slices and wasabi and accompanied by soy sauce.
Serves 2
Note: It is essential to use a live fresh lobster to obtain the correct texture for this dish. Frozen lobster flesh becomes rubbery, dry and tough and is not suitable for eating raw.

Lobsters from Sydney have green coloured shells, strong flavour and firm flesh. Victorian and Tasmanian lobsters are more delicately flavoured and the flesh is more tender. The outer shell is pale red.

All types of lobster are suitable for isebi-no-ikezukuri as long as they are very fresh.

Mori-awase *(Combination sashimi)*

Mori-awase can be presented using whole snapper (sugata-zukuri), tuna, garfish etc., also whole green lobster (ise-ebi) with cuttlefish and abalone. This is a very attractive dish and is suitable for large groups and entertaining.

Sashimi fish fillets and shellfish sashimi in the shell can be served on ice with a flower arrangement or a vegetable carving (mukimono) for a spectacular effect.

Katsuo-no-tataki *(Salt-grilled bonito)*

Bonito is naturally a strongly flavoured fish but prepared in this way it has quite a subtle flavour.

1 medium-sized bonito
  (katsuo)
1 onion, thinly sliced into
  rings

1 dried, red chilli, chopped
1 tablespoon finely
  chopped seaweed
3 tablespoons salt

Fillet bonito and discard head, tail and bones. Skewer fillets lengthways, skin side up, in 2 or 3 places. Cover skin with a layer of salt and grill on high heat for 2 minutes. Remove from griller and plunge into icy cold water for a minute or so.

While the fish is immersed in the water rub the salt from the skin and remove skewers. Remove bonito fillets from the water and cut each fillet in two lengthways. Remove any large bones from the fish and slice it sashimi style.

Arrange fish on a serving plate. Combine onion rings with chilli and seaweed and spread over the sliced fish.
Serves 2

Katsuo-no-tataki
(salt-grilled bonito)

Isebi-no-ikezukuri (live green
lobster)

Niku-no-tataki *(Chopped beef)*

Beef sashimi is also popular in Japan today despite the high price of beef. It is simple to prepare and delicious to eat.

1 × 300 g piece eye fillet of beef
2 cups white vinegar
½ cup sugar
2 shallots, finely chopped
1 × 2 cm piece green ginger, grated

Thinly slice beef and then cut into small squares. Combine vinegar, sugar, shallots and ginger in a bowl and marinate meat in this mixture for a few seconds. Remove beef from marinade and serve on a platter accompanied by shredded cucumber or grated horseradish.
Serves 2

Niku-no-sashimi *(Sliced beef)*

1 fresh eye fillet of beef

Using a very sharp knife, slice beef thinly, sushi style. The eye fillet may be frozen for one hour prior to slicing in order to obtain the thinnest possible slices.

To serve niku-no-sashimi, arrange beef slices decoratively on a serving dish. For variation in presentation, the slices may be moulded into the shape of a flower.

Niku-no-sashimi is served with soy sauce, wasabi (green mustard) and chopped shallots. Strongly flavoured dipping sauces and vegetables are not served as they may mask the subtle flavour of the raw beef.

Although raw meat is commonly eaten in Japan it is only recently starting to become acceptable in the west.

Niku-no-sashimi is a simple dish to prepare and lends itself to entertaining either small or large groups of people without undue fuss.
Serves 4

Aji-no-tataki *(Chopped yellowtail)*

5 medium-sized fresh whole yellowtail
2 cups white vinegar
½ cup sugar
2 shallot stalks, finely chopped
1 × 2 cm piece green ginger, grated

Clean, scale and fillet the yellowtail and remove skin and bones. Chop flesh into small dice. Combine the vinegar, sugar, shallots and ginger in a bowl and marinate fish in this mixture for 10 seconds.

Remove fish from marinade and using the back of a knife flatten the fish slightly. Serve with head, tail and bones as in recipe for sugata-zukuri.
Serves 5

Sayori *(Garfish)*

3 medium-sized garfish

Clean, fillet and skin the garfish, discarding head, tail and bones as illustrated in the step-by-step photographs. Once each garfish is filleted into 2 pieces, cut down the centre of each fillet so you have 4 fillets. (It is important when cutting down the centre of the fillets that you cut in the middle of the stripe marked on the flesh.)

Using the fingers, roll each fillet into a snail shape, ensuring that the stripe on the flesh is facing upwards. The two-toned fish fillet looks beautiful when presented in this way.

As an alternative to this method of presentation, each fillet can be tied into a loose knot.

To serve sayori, arrange each fillet on a serving plate and garnish with a prawn, wasabi and thin lemon slices. Sayori may also be accompanied by a favourite dipping sauce.
Serves 3

1. Using a long-bladed fish knife, cut into fish below head and carefully slice a long fillet off backbone.

2. Turn fish over and cut a similar fillet from other side.

3. Peel skin from fillets.

Sayori (garfish) sashimi

Sugata-zukuri *(Whole snapper)*

1 medium-sized whole
    snapper
1 lemon

Clean, scale and fillet the snapper into 2 large pieces. Remove skin from only one of the fillets. Slice the skinned fillet sashimi style. Place a piece of kitchen paper on the skin side of the remaining fillet and pour boiling water over it. This method is called shimo-furi and removes excess oiliness from the fish. Remove the paper and slice fillet with the skin still on into sashimi slices.

Sugata-zukuri means whole snapper, so on presentation of this dish, the head, tail and bones are used as a bed on which the sashimi sliced flesh is arranged. The lemon is sliced and arranged between the pieces of snapper, not only as a garnish but to give additional flavour to the dish.

In Japan sugata-zukuri is a popular dish for special occasions such as weddings and all joyous celebrations.
Serves 4

Sugata-zukuri (whole snapper)

Maguro *(Tuna fish)*

In Sydney's fish markets the yellow-fin tuna is readily available and is especially recommended for this dish. In Australia there are a number of different species of tuna fish. The blue-fin tuna comes from Port Lincoln in Adelaide, black-fin tuna from Queensland and striped tuna is available throughout New South Wales. Australia is very fortunate to have tuna fish in such abundance. In Japanese waters all species of tuna fish are decreasing in numbers and imported tuna from Australia, Canada and Africa is becoming increasingly important.

It is absolutely necessary to use fresh fish when preparing sashimi. All sashimi is served with soy sauce and wasabi (green mustard) and with either thin shreds of horseradish (tsuma) or cucumber and shredded vegetables.

300 g fresh tuna
horseradish (tsuma)
1 tablespoon wasabi
2 tablespoons soy sauce

Slice tuna thinly, sashimi style. Shred horseradish and arrange on a serving plate. Arrange slices of tuna over the horseradish and serve accompanied by a dipping sauce made with wasabi and soy sauce. Basil seeds are sometimes added to the sauce for extra flavour.
Serves 4

Maguro (tuna fish)

Buri *(Kingfish)*

1 kg fresh kingfish
100 g daikon
½ cup soy sauce
1 teaspoon wasabi
basil seeds

Slice the kingfish thinly, sashimi style. Shred the daikon and place on a plate. Arrange the slices of kingfish over the daikon and serve accompanied by a dipping sauce made of wasabi and soy sauce combined. Basil seeds may be added to the dipping sauce for extra flavour.
Serves 6

Note: Kan-buri is a winter season kingfish. This is the best season to eat the kingfish as it contains a higher fat content than normal. During this time it also tastes sweeter. In Japan, kingfish are cultivated on special farms and the fish are called hama-chi. A young kingfish is called inada whilst the mature ones are called buri.

Kingfish in between the young and old stages are called warasa.

Dipping Sauces
Ponzu sauce

1 cup lemon or lime juice, strained
⅓ cup plus 2 tablespoons rice vinegar
1 cup dark soy sauce
2 tablespoons tamari sauce
3 tablespoons mirin, alcohol burnt off

10 g (small handful) dried bonito flakes (hana-katsuo)
5 cm square giant kelp (konbu)

Combine ingredients and let stand for 24 hours. Strain through muslin and mature for three months in a cool dark place or in the refrigerator. Keeps indefinitely but really best used within twelve months.

Yields 2½ cups
Note: A combination of lemon and lime juice can be substituted for the lemon. In Japan sudachi citron or other very acid citrus fruits are used.

Shoga-joyu *(Ginger soy sauce)*

1 tablespoon root ginger, finely grated
½ cup soy sauce

Prepare just before using as it tends to lose its pungency and aroma.

Yields ½ cup

Goma-joyu *(Sesame soy sauce)*

2 tablespoons white sesame seeds
½ cup Tosa soy sauce (or use dark soy sauce plus ½

tablespoon mirin from which alcohol has been burnt off)

Toast sesame seeds in a dry pan till golden and grind to a flaky paste in a grinding bowl. Stir in the soy sauce and mirin.

Yields ¾ cup

Bainiku-joyu *(Plum soy sauce)*

2 tablespoons pickled plums (bainiku, available

canned), sieved
½ cup Tosa soy sauce

Combine ingredients. This keeps well in the refrigerator.

Yields ¾ cup

Wasabi-joyu *(Horseradish soy sauce)*

1 tablespoon wasabi
½ cup Tosa soy sauce

Combine ingredients. Store until required for use.

Yields ½ cup

Goma-dare *(Sesame sauce)*

85 g white sesame seeds
¾ cup dashi
6 tablespoons dark soy sauce
2 tablespoons mirin wine
1 tablespoon sugar
1–2 tablespoons saké
½ cup finely chopped shallots
1 cup finely grated daikon (white radish)

In a dry, heavy frypan toast the white sesame seeds over medium heat till golden brown. They burn easily, so keep them moving by shaking the pan.
Transfer warm toasted seeds to a suribachi (Japanese grinding bowl) or pestle and mortar and grind till flaky. Add the remaining ingredients and

dilute with dashi, mixing well between additions. Sprinkle with shallots and fold through daikon before serving.
The sauce may be stored in a tightly sealed container in the refrigerator for up to 3 days but is at its best when freshly made. Stir before serving in case some of the sesame has settled to the bottom.

Yields 2½ cups

Age-Mono and Tempura

Deep-fried Foods

*T*he technique of deep-frying was introduced to Japan centuries ago by the Chinese and Europeans. But typically, the Japanese have developed this method of cooking (age-mono) to its utmost refinement.

There are several methods of Japanese-style deep-frying, the best known of which is tempura — batter-coated deep-frying. There are tempura bars and restaurants throughout Japan where these dishes are cooked to perfection. But they are, for all their delicacy, fairly easy to cook in an average Australian kitchen. The oil for frying should be very light — polyunsaturated vegetable oil is best — and perfectly clean. A few drops of sesame oil can be added for flavour if liked.

Ebi no-somen (noodle-coated prawns)

Sayori nanban-zuke *(Deep-fried garfish)*

5 medium-sized garfish
oil for deep frying
2 cups white vinegar
2 ½ tablespoons sugar
pinch salt
3 tablespoons mirin wine
5 whole dried red chillies
1 onion, sliced
1 shallot stalk, chopped

Clean, scale and gut garfish. Pass a skewer through each garfish beginning at the tail and finishing at the head so that it forms an S-shape. Drop each fish into hot oil and fry until golden and crisp. Remove from oil and drain.

Combine the vinegar,

sugar, salt, mirin, whole chillies, onion and shallot in a bowl. Marinate the fried garfish in this sweet and sour sauce for 1 hour to allow the flavours to penetrate the flesh.

Remove fish from marinade and arrange on serving dish. Garnish with the

vegetables from the marinade as well as some grated horseradish and thin lemon slices.
Serves 5

Tonkatsu no-ankake *(Deep-fried pork fillets)*

This deep-fried breaded pork cutlet is as famous as tempura, and like tempura, was originally introduced from the west. The Japanese version has been derived from the European 'schnitzel' but whereas the latter is shallow-fried, tonkatsu is always deep-fried. It is one of the most popular everyday dishes in Japan and a meal consisting of deep-fried pork on a bed of cabbage with a bowl of rice, a soup and a side dish of pickles costs about 1,000 yen, or $4.00 in a modest restaurant.

This dish is a lot heavier and more substantial than tempura, almost Germanic in style. Its great advantage is that it is inexpensive and very filling. Prepared with a good cut of lean pork it can also be very tender and succulent. Tonkatsu is usually served accompanied by a thick sauce.

300 g pork fillet
salt and pepper
50 g plain flour
4 egg yolks
100 g breadcrumbs
½ cup Tonkatsu sauce
  (bottled)
oil for deep frying

Slice pork fillets into half centimetre thick slices. Flatten each fillet with a mallet. Sprinkle with salt and pepper and allow to stand for 5 minutes.

Coat the seasoned fillets in plain flour, dip into the beaten

egg yolks then coat with breadcrumbs, pressing firmly into the pork.

Fry crumbed pork fillets in hot oil until golden. Remove and drain on kitchen paper. Slice each fillet neatly into 2.5 cm lengths and arrange on

a bed of finely shredded cabbage or simply garnish with fine shreds of dried seaweed.

Tonkatsu sauce and mustard are used as dipping sauces to accompany the pork.
Serves 2
Note: When deep frying, ½ cup of sesame oil may be added for extra flavour.

If Tonkatsu sauce is unavailable substitute Worcestershire sauce or a home-made sauce consisting of 1 tablespoon sugar, ¼ cup tomato sauce, 1 teaspoon soy sauce and a sprinkling of nutmeg and paprika.

**Tonkatsu no-ankake
(deep-fried pork fillets)**

Hirame no-ankake *(Lemon sole with sauce)*

3 medium-sized lemon sole
oil for deep-frying
½ cup cornflour
½ cup soy sauce
½ tablespoon mirin wine
½ cup dashi (see stocks
   chapter)
pinch salt
1 tablespoon grated ginger
250 g bean curd, diced

Clean and scale the sole. Using a sharp knife cut down the middle of the sole through to the bone. Then make a cut at right angles, along base of head. Gently lift and roll the flesh outwards on both sides exposing the backbone. Heat oil, carefully slide fish in and cook until crisp and golden brown. Remove from oil and drain. Repeat with remaining lemon sole. Keep sole warm.

To make the sauce (ankake) combine the cornflour, soy sauce, mirin, dashi and salt. Place in a saucepan and simmer over gentle heat until thick. Finally squeeze juice from grated ginger and add to the sauce.

Gently combine the sauce with the diced bean curd and chopped shallots. Arrange the fish on plates and pour the sauce into the opening of each lemon sole. Garnish with lemon slices and a strip of cucumber peel.
Serves 3–4

Hirame no-ankake
(lemon sole with sauce)

Masu nanban-zuke *(Deep-fried whole trout)*

3 whole trout
oil for deep frying
2 cups white vinegar
2½ tablespoons sugar
pinch salt
3 tablespoons mirin wine
5 whole dried red chillies
1 onion, sliced
1 shallot stalk, chopped

Clean, scale and remove backbone from each trout. Thread trout onto skewers, shaping to form an S. Drop each trout into hot oil and fry until golden and crisp. Remove from oil and drain.

Combine the vinegar, sugar, salt, mirin, whole chillies, sliced onion and chopped shallot in a bowl. Marinate the fried fish in this sweet and sour sauce for 1 hour, to allow flavours to penetrate the flesh.

Remove fish from the marinade and arrange on a serving dish. Garnish with dried red chillies, sliced onion, a ball of grated horseradish and green leaves from any flower.
Serves 3

Tatsuta-age *(Deep-fried chicken)*

200 g chicken breasts
½ cup soy sauce
1½ tablespoons sugar
¼ cup mirin wine
50 g cornflour (katakuri-ko)
pinch salt
pinch ground basil (yukari)
1 sheet dried seaweed (ao-
   nori)
oil for frying

Fillet the chicken breasts leaving skin on. Chop each fillet into 5 cm squares. Combine soy sauce, mirin, salt and basil to make marinade. Place chicken pieces into marinade and leave for 10 minutes. Remove chicken from marinade and drain.

Finely chop the seaweed and combine with the cornflour. Roll each piece of chicken in the cornflour, coating evenly. Deep fry chicken until golden. Drain.

Serve on a plate accompanied by hot English mustard.
Serves 2–3

Meat kushi-age

This is a modern Japanese-style dish, very good for parties.

200 g eye fillet
100 g Cheddar cheese
2 shallot stalks
1 carrot
1 packet Japanese
  breadcrumbs
100 g plain flour
2 egg yolks

Slice fillet thinly. Cut cheese and shallots into 7 cm lengths. Peel and cut carrot into 7 cm julienne strips and blanch in boiling water until tender.

Place a piece of cheese, shallot and carrot onto the centre of a slice of fillet and roll up tightly. Secure each roll with bamboo skewers.

Combine flour with egg yolks to make a batter. Dip each roll into the batter and then coat with breadcrumbs. Deep-fry each roll until centre is cooked and outside browned. Remove from oil and drain.

Using a sharp knife cut the rolls into rounds 2.5 cm thick and arrange on a plate. Serve with Tonkatsu sauce or with yellow mustard and soy sauce. Serves 2–3
Note: Fish is a good substitute for the beef and can be served in the same way.

Fish kushi-age

Kesyo-age *(Dressed-up prawns)*

5 large green prawns
150 g domyoji (coarse rice
  flour)
1 piece seaweed
oil for deep-frying

Batter
1 egg yolk
1 cup iced water
1 cup flour

Shell and devein the prawns. Make 4 incisions into the undersection of each prawn and open up the cuts to straighten.

Combine batter ingredients in a bowl. Wrap a small piece of seaweed around the end of the prawn tail and dip each prawn into the batter. Do not coat the seaweed nor the tail with the batter. Coat the prawns with domyoji.

Heat oil and fry prawns until light golden in colour. Remove from oil and drain.

Arrange prawns in a dish on a folded sheet of rice paper. Garnish with a deep fried seaweed bow, grated ginger and horseradish. Serves 2–3

Kesyo-age (dressed-up prawns)

Ebi *(Prawns)*

Prawn tempura is well known throughout the world. The key to a successful ebi is short, intense cooking — overcooking causes toughness. Ebi must be full of flavour, crisp on the outside and tender inside.

**5 large green prawns
1 piece dried seaweed
extra flour for coating
oil for deep-frying
1 cup flour
1 cup iced water
1 egg yolk**

Shell and devein prawns. Cut 4 incisions into the undersection of each prawn and straighten them out to open up the cuts. Tie a piece of seaweed around the base of the tail. Coat each prawn with flour, leaving the seaweed and tail uncoated.

Heat the oil. Combine flour, water and yolk to make batter. Dip each prawn into the batter (leaving seaweed and tail uncoated) and slip into the hot oil. Fry until golden, remove and drain. Arrange on rice paper and serve.

Serves 2

Note: Ebi is sometimes served with lemon and salt. A tempura sauce and grated horseradish may also accompany this dish.

1. Combine flour, egg yolk and iced water to make batter.

2. Dip each prawn in flour then in batter.

3. Drop into hot oil.

4. Fry until golden, remove and drain.

Ebi (prawn tempura)

Ebi no-somen *(Noodle-coated prawns)*

5 large green prawns
2 small bunches somen (thin
　noodles)
1 small piece dried seaweed
oil for deep-frying

Batter
2 egg yolks
2 cups iced water
2 cups flour

Shell and remove veins from prawns. Make a shallow incision into the underside of prawns and open up the cuts to straighten them.

　Place egg yolks, flour and water in a bowl and blend together using chopsticks. Heat oil. Place noodles on a board.

　Dip each prawn into the batter and press into the somen so they adhere to and cover the prawn. Wrap a 2 cm strip of seaweed around the centre of the prawn and gently slide into the hot oil. Cook until noodles are golden brown and serve hot.

　Arrange on a plate and serve with a dipping sauce and lemon garnish.
Serves 2–3

1. Roll each battered prawn in somen.

2. Press somen onto prawn so they adhere.

3. Wrap a strip of seaweed round centre of each prawn.

4. Drop into hot oil, fry until golden and drain.

Ika *(Deep-fried calamari)*

1 squid
1 tablespoon sesame seeds
1 shallot stalk
oil for deep-frying

Batter
2 egg yolks
2 cups iced water
2 cups flour

Clean and skin the squid as shown for cuttlefish (p. 24) Use a sharp knife to cut the squid tube into rings.

　In a bowl combine the egg yolks, water and flour using chopsticks. Allow to rest 5 minutes. Chop shallot stalk finely. Add the sesame seeds, chopped shallots, and squid rings to the batter and mix. Heat oil and, using chopsticks, place 5 or 6 rings into the oil at a time. When golden remove from the oil and drain.

　Serve, skewered, on Japanese folded rice paper garnished with lemon, carrot and seaweed.
Serves 2–3

Yasai kaki-age *(Deep-fried cuttlefish)*

2 shallot stalks
1 medium-sized cuttlefish
1 carrot
oil for deep-frying

Batter
2 egg yolks
2 cups iced water
2 cups flour

Chop shallots finely. Clean and skin cuttlefish (see p.24). Using a sharp knife, chop the cuttlefish finely. Peel and slice carrot into 7 cm long julienne pieces.

　In a large bowl combine the egg yolks, iced water and flour, using chopsticks. Add carrots, shallots and cuttlefish to the batter and mix well. Heat oil. Using 2 dessert-spoons, take some of the batter into one of the spoons and drop into the hot oil with the aid of a second spoon. When the yasai float to the surface of the oil, they are cooked.

　Remove from oil and drain on kitchen paper before serving. Serve on a plate with golden fried mushrooms, seaweed bows and lemon wedges, accompanied by soy sauce in a small bowl.
Serves 2

Yasai kaki-age (deep-fried cuttlefish)

Ika (deep-fried calamari)

Pot-Cooking

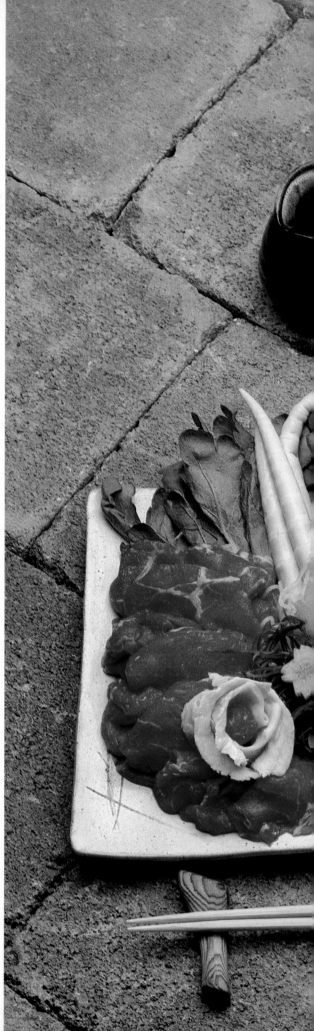

Japanese pot-cooked dishes are tasty, fairly substantial and warming. They make a satisfying country-style meal in the tradition of the daubes of provincial France and the stews of the British Isles.

But there the resemblance ends. Instead of long, slow cooking in the European tradition small morsels of food are cooked very quickly in a steaming pot of broth. A small charcoal brazier or spirit burner keeps the pot bubbling at the table and diners select pieces of food from beautifully arranged platters of meat, fish, chicken and vegetables. These are dipped into the pot with chopsticks to cook, and removed and eaten after a minute or so. The broth may be served separately in bowls at the end of the meal.

When preparing ingredients for pot-cooked dishes cut food into pieces of such a size that cooking time will be about equal. Use twice the volume of vegetables to meat and fish; this is nutritionally sound and looks more decorative on a platter.

Sukiyaki

Zaru soba *(Noodles in a basket)*

These chilled buckwheat noodles are traditionally served in square, slatted, bamboo boxes accompanied by a cold, clear, piquant dipping sauce. Wasabi (horseradish) and finely shredded shallot are mixed into the sauce for added flavour. Every region has a unique way of serving zaru soba. It is an ideal dish for a hot summer day.

225 g dried buckwheat noodles (soba)
3 cups noodle dipping sauce (following recipe)
¼ cup toasted nori seaweed, finely shredded

Condiments
1 teaspoon wasabi
5 tablespoons finely shredded shallot
4 tablespoons daikon (white radish), finely grated

Cook noodles in plenty of boiling water until just tender. Remove immediately and plunge into cold water to remove excess starch. Drain well and divide among 4 plates.

Sprinkle nori shreds on each serving of noodles. Serve the dipping sauce in individual, small bowls. Place spicy garnishes in serving dishes and allow diners to help themselves.

To eat, mix a dab of wasabi horseradish and about 1 tablespoon finely shredded shallot or daikon into the dipping sauce. Pick up noodles with chopsticks, dip into the sauce and eat.
Serves 4

Tsuke-jiru *(Noodle dipping sauce)*

Primarily for soba noodles.

2½ cups dashi
½ cup plus 2 tablespoons dark soy sauce
4 tablespoons mirin wine
1 teaspoon sugar
30 g (about 3 cups loose) dried bonito flakes

In a small pan combine all ingredients except bonito flakes and bring just to the boil over medium heat. Stir in bonito flakes and immediately remove from heat. Wait 10 seconds till flakes are thoroughly soaked then strain. Let liquid cool to room temperature before use.

This dipping sauce can be prepared in advance. In a covered container in the refrigerator it will keep for several months.
Yields 3 cups

Nabeyaki udon *(Noodles in the pot)*

This is essentially a one-portion version of a noodle sukiyaki. Use small heatproof casseroles.

450 g dried udon noodles
4 green prawns
1 cake fish paste (kamaboko)
4 fresh or dried mushrooms
12 small sprigs watercress or young spinach leaves
4–6 cups noodle broth
4 eggs

Boil noodles as directed on the pack. Rinse well under cold water to remove excess starch. Clean, shell and devein the prawns but leave the tails attached. Cut fish paste into ¾ cm slices. Trim and thinly slice the mushrooms. Wash and dry the spinach or watercress.

Keep noodle broth at a gentle simmer. Divide noodles into portions, placing them in the base of four individual casserole dishes. On top of the noodles arrange the other ingredients. Ladle 1½ cups hot broth into each dish. Cover and boil over medium heat for 4–5 minutes.

Make a small well in the centre of each nest of noodles.

Break an egg gently into the cavity. Re-cover and simmer until egg is cooked but the yolk still soft. Serve immediately with chopsticks and a porcelain spoon.
Serves 4
Note: Any number of other ingredients may be added, for example small pieces of chicken or shallots.

Kake-jiru *(Noodle broth)*

Use with soba or udon noodles. This is a basic recipe which can be adapted to individual tastes.

8 cups dashi
2 teaspoons salt
3 tablespoons dark soy sauce
3 tablespoons light soy sauce
2 tablespoons sugar
2 tablespoons mirin wine

Bring dashi to the boil and season with the other ingredients. Remove from heat and strain. Keep at a low simmer and use piping hot.

You can prepare this broth well in advance, cool to room temperature, then refrigerate in a covered container — it will keep for up to three days. When using the broth for soba noodles you can increase the quantity of dark soy sauce to taste.
Yields 8 cups

Kake-udon *(Noodles in broth)*

This is certainly one of the simplest noodles dishes to prepare. It consists of hot udon noodles in a deep earthenware bowl, almost covered with tasty broth and completed with a fine sprinkling of shredded shallots.

450 g dried udon noodles
4 heaped tablespoons finely shredded shallots
6 cups noodle broth
seven-spice mixture

Boil noodles according to pack instructions. Drain and rinse well under cold running water to remove excess starch. Reheat cooked noodles by plunging into boiling water.

Keep noodle broth at a gentle simmer. Divide noodles into portions in warmed noodle bowls. Garnish with shallots. Ladle 1½ cups broth into each bowl and serve immediately. Sprinkle on seven-spice mixture to taste.
Serves 4

Sukiyaki

Sukiyaki is a world famous Japanese dish consisting of thinly sliced beef fillets and an array of Japanese vegetables. It can be cooked and served at the table. The many colours in this dish are a treat for the eye and help stimulate the appetite.

600 g eye fillet *or* scotch fillet
½ Japanese cabbage
4 shallots
2 bamboo shoots (take-noko)
1 carrot
125 g tofu
100 g piece suet
3 Japanese mushrooms (shiitake)
100 g rice noodles (vermicelli)
4 spinach leaves *or* watercress sprigs
2 baby corn cobs
some Japanese hill vegetables (carrots, mushrooms, daikon, bracken etc.)
3 raw eggs

Sauce (Warishita)
1 cup soy sauce
¼ cup mirin wine
½ cup sugar
pinch salt
1 piece dried kelp *or* ½ cup fish stock (dashi)

Thinly slice the fillet of beef. Slice the Japanese cabbage into 5 cm pieces. Cut the shallots into 7.5 cm lengths and thinly slice the bamboo shoots. Cut the carrots into fine shreds and cut the tofu into 2.5 cm squares.

Cut the suet into long thin pieces and form into the shape of a blooming flower, as shown in the step-by-step illustrations for sukiyaki.

Place mushrooms into warm water and soak for 10 minutes.

Soak the vermicelli in a bowl of warm water for 30 minutes until tender.

Roll the spinach leaves up and cut into 7.5 cm lengths. Cut the baby corn cobs in half and set aside. (If using any hilly vegetables, simply cut into desired shapes and use fresh.)

To make the sukiyaki sauce (warishita) combine the soy sauce, mirin, salt and dried kelp in a saucepan and heat for 30 minutes on low heat.

Arrange all the ingredients beautifully on a plate.

Heat the frypan and place the suet flower in it. Use this to grease the base of the pan. Gently fry the beef pieces and the shallots. When tender, pour over some of the warishita sauce then add remaining ingredients (except the eggs) to the pan and continue to cook gently until tender. Repeat this cooking process until all ingredients are used.

During the frying process some saké or water may be added to the pan to prevent excessive flavour development of the warishita and to maintain a balance of flavours throughout the cooking.

To serve sukiyaki, place the beaten eggs in a bowl and use for dipping the sukiyaki pieces into. The raw egg is optional and not always used by western people. Sukiyaki is served from the pot into small bowls or plates.
Serves 4

1. Thinly slice fillet.

2. Place suet flower in frypan.

3. Add beef pieces and shallots.

4. Add remaining ingredients.

5. Pour over warishita sauce.

Ishi kari-nabe *(Salmon nabe)*

1 medium-sized salmon
250 g kinugashi tofu (bean curd)
½ Japanese cabbage
12 Japanese dried mushrooms (shiitake)
8 cups seasoned dashi
2 × 5 cm pieces bamboo shoot
4 tablespoons Japanese soy sauce
¼ cup mirin wine or saké
pinch salt

Clean and scale salmon. Remove fins, tail and head. Slice into 5 cm thick cutlets.

Cut tofu into 6 squares. Shred the cabbage coarsely, approximately 5 cm wide.

Soak the shiitake mushrooms in warm water for 10 minutes.

Place all ingredients into the pot and add the dashi, mirin or saké, soy sauce and salt.

Place over a medium heat and simmer, covered, for 15 minutes.

Turn the salmon pieces over and simmer a further 15 minutes or until tender. When cooked, serve salmon in the pot accompanied by a variety of sauces such as goma-dare or ponzu (p.31).

Fresh salmon is not as readily available in Australia as it is in Japan. Frozen salmon may be substituted.

The head, fins and tail can be reserved and used to make an excellent fish stock.
Serves 3–4

Uosuki *(Fish sukiyaki)*

5 large green king prawns
1 small snapper
1 small flathead
½ small green lobster
5 scallops
5 pipis
5 mussels
5 oysters
1 medium crab, uncooked
250 g bean curd (tofu)
5 large leaves Japanese cabbage
¼ bunch shallots
1 cup dashi
1 quantity warishita sauce (p.43)

Shell, clean and dry the king prawns. Clean, scale and fillet the fish and slice it thinly, sashimi style. Reserve the snapper head. Clean and shell remaining shellfish.

Blanch cabbage leaves in boiling water for 2 minutes.

Cut shallots into 7.5 cm lengths. Lay a cabbage leaf out flat, place a piece of shallot and a prawn in the centre and roll up tightly. Cut into 5 cm pieces and set aside.

Dice the bean curd into 2.5 cm squares. Carefully

arrange all ingredients in the pot, including the snapper head.

Pour the cold dashi into the pot followed by the warishita sauce. Place pot over a low flame and cook until seafood is tender. Uosuki is served from the pot accompanied by raw beaten eggs in small bowls.
Serves 5
Note: White fish such as Spanish mackerel, snapper, barramundi and jewfish should be used for this dish. Red fish

such as bonito and tuna are not suitable.

Shabu-shabu

Chopstick-held morsels of raw meat and vegetables are gently dipped into a steaming broth, poached, literally only for seconds, then removed. The paper-thin slices are succulently tender and are enhanced with spicy dipping sauces. Guests dip into a flame-proof casserole of broth at the table. When all the meat and

vegetables have been eaten, noodles are added to the broth and a bowl is served to each diner. In Japan, shabu-shabu is a very popular party dish. Its name derives from the swishing sound made by chopsticks in the broth.

1 kg prime-quality beef or lamb, cut into paper-thin slices across the grain of the meat
12 shiitake mushrooms, trimmed
10 shallots, cut diagonally into 4 cm lengths
7 Chinese cabbage leaves, washed, parboiled, refreshed and torn into bite-sized pieces
1 bunch edible chrysanthemum leaves, washed, trimmed and cut in half
2 cakes tofu (bean curd), cut into 4 cm squares

8–10 small pieces wheat gluten (fu), soaked for 5 minutes in tepid water
225 g bamboo shoot, cut into half-moon slices about ¾ cm thick
10 cm square kelp (konbu), slashed in a few places to release flavour

Arrange all ingredients attractively on a large round platter so that each piece can be easily picked up with chopsticks.

Place the square of kelp in a large donabe casserole or Mongolian hot-pot. Fill the casserole two-thirds full of water. Bring to boil, then simmer gently for four minutes. Each diner should have chopsticks and two dipping bowls. Pieces of vegetable and meat are picked up from the platter and swished to and fro in the simmering broth till just

tender. Skim the broth occasionally to keep it free from foam.

Serve with ponzu sauce and sesame sauce (p.31).
Serves 6

Mizu-taki *(Chicken one-pot)*

Mizu-taki is a hearty, warming dish which is initially prepared at the kitchen stove and then assembled for prolonged, gentle simmering and mingling of flavours in a donabe at the table. Mizu-taki (literally 'water-simmered') is the poultry version of chirinabe or fish one-pot. It makes a very economical family meal as it uses many parts of a chicken. Vegetables are added from a beautifully arranged platter and before serving the foods are dipped in a spicy ponzu sauce. This is followed by a course of rice and pickles.

1 × 1.25 kg chicken or
  chicken pieces
10 cm square kelp (konbu)
6 leaves Chinese cabbage
12 shiitake mushrooms,
  cleaned and trimmed
2 carrots, peeled and cut
  into decorative slices
40 g dried harusame
  filaments, soaked in hot
  water
1 bunch young spinach,
  washed and trimmed

Condiments
Ponzu sauce (p.31)
4–6 tablespoons red maple
  radish
4–6 tablespoons finely
  chopped shallots
slivers of yuzu citron or
  lemon rind

Chop chicken, including skin and bones into 5 cm pieces. Place in a saucepan and add the kelp which has been slashed several times to release its flavour. Fill pan with 5 litres water. Bring to boil and just before water reaches boiling point remove the kelp. Simmer for 20–30 minutes. Strain chicken from broth and keep moistened with a little of the liquid. Reserve remaining broth for use at the table.

Blanch the cabbage leaves for 2 minutes; refresh. Drain, pat dry and tear into bite-sized pieces.

Cut decorative crosses in the top of each mushroom cap. If shiitake are unavailable small cap mushrooms can be substituted. If these are very large, cut in half.

Arrange the vegetables attractively on a large platter. The chicken should remain separate. The table should be set with individual dipping bowls, a couple of small dishes of ponzu sauce and dishes filled with spicy condiments. Chopsticks should be placed at each setting.

Fill a donabe casserole three-quarters full of reserved stock. Place on a portable gas flame at the table. Heat till broth is gently simmering, then slowly add chicken and vegetables. Simmer ingredients for a few minutes until just tender and heated through. Dip foods into ponzu sauce to eat.
Serves 6
Note: Many different kinds of vegetables such as bamboo shoots, leeks and grilled bean curd can be used.

Udon-suki

A variety of ingredients, good udon noodles and a flavoursome broth all contribute to the making of this very popular Osakan dish.

Fresh noodles can be made if udon are unavailable. Homemade noodles are always superior to the dried varieties. The cooked noodles are arranged on a platter and then topped with the other ingredients, which are generally eaten first. The noodles are unveiled and folded through the broth towards the end of the meal.

450 g dried udon noodles
2 cakes deep-fried or grilled
  bean curd
1 cake kamaboko (fish
  paste)
½ cup bamboo shoots,
  sliced thinly into half-
  moon shapes
2 fillets anago eel (if
  available) grilled and cut
  into 6 pieces
6 green prawns, parboiled
  and deveined with tails
  intact
8 stalks trefoil (mitsuba) or
  spinach stalks, cut into
  halves or thirds
12 fresh mushrooms, with
  decoratively carved
  crosses on each cap
6 pieces mochi (glutinous
  rice cake) baked for 5
  minutes to allow for
  swelling, then cut into
  4 cm squares

10 cm length daikon (white
  radish) boiled and cut into
  1.5 cm rounds
450 g spinach leaves,
  blanched, refreshed and
  cut into 5 cm lengths
500 g dark chicken meat
  (thigh) with skin, cut into
  4 cm squares

Broth
2 litres dashi
½ cup mirin wine
1 cup dark soy sauce
2 teaspoons salt

Condiments
4 tablespoons finely grated
  root ginger
6 tablespoons finely
  chopped shallots
seven-spice mixture
  (shichimi)
lemon wedges *or* strained
  juice 1 lemon

Cook udon noodles according to packet instructions. Do not overcook or they will become limp and mushy.

Place the dashi and other broth ingredients into a donabe or similar flameproof casserole and bring to a simmer over medium heat. This can be done at the table.

When broth is simmering each guest adds the seafood ingredients, then follows with the vegetables. Each diner should have an individual dipping bowl filled with broth at the commencement of the meal. Diners add spicy condiments of their choice to the broth.

Additional dashi (stock) can be added to the casserole throughout the meal to keep it clear and thin. When the broth is heavily flavoured the noodles are added and served immediately. Chopsticks are the ideal cooking and eating implement for udon-suki.
Serves 6

Mizu-taki (chicken one-pot)

Sansai nabe *(Vegetables with bean curd)*

Sansai makes use of some of the unusual vegetables which grow in the hills of Japan such as bracken, fungus and golden mushrooms.

5 pieces bracken
5 golden mushrooms
3 Japanese cabbage leaves
1 spinach leaf
5 × 7.5 cm carrot sticks
5 pieces lotus root
5 × 5 cm pieces bamboo shoot
5 marron (sweet chestnuts)
250 g kinugashi tofu
2 shallot stalks
4 tablespoons Japanese soy sauce

¼ cup mirin wine
8 cups seasoned dashi (see stocks chapter)

Blanch cabbage leaves and spinach in boiling water for 2 minutes. Place carrots into boiling salted water and cook until tender. Drain.

Place the spinach leaf and a carrot stick onto a cabbage leaf and then using a bamboo mat, roll up lengthwise and press into a square shape. Cut into 5 cm pieces (called hakusai-maki).

Arrange all remaining ingredients, including the squares, in a pot. Add the dashi, mirin wine and soy sauce and cover. Simmer gently on low heat for 20 minutes.

Sansai can be served with finely grated ginger and ponzu sauce (p.31).

Chirinabe *(Fish one-pot)*

Chirinabe uses whole chunks of fish — skin, bones and all. The broth in which the fish and vegetables are simmered must be well flavoured. Use the fish head too; the flesh is very tasty and considered a delicacy in Japan, usually reserved for the guest of honour. The raw fish and fresh vegetables are brought to the table decoratively arranged on platters and guests cook whatever they like in a kelp-flavoured broth.

Chirinabe is eaten with tart ponzu sauce and other spicy condiments served in individual dipping bowls. Follow the meal with steamed white rice and broth.

1.5 kg firm white fish, such as bream or snapper, cut crosswise into 5 cm chunks (reserve the head for broth)
6 Chinese cabbage leaves, blanched, refreshed and torn into bite-sized pieces
1 bunch spinach, prepared as for cabbage
1 bunch edible

chrysanthemum leaves, washed, trimmed and cut in half
500 g whole enokitake mushrooms (if available), trimmed
2 cakes tofu (bean curd), each cut into six pieces
8–10 small pieces wheat gluten (fu), rinsed, soaked

for 5 minutes and squeezed dry
10 cm square giant kelp (konbu), slashed several times to release flavour
1 carrot, cut into ¾ cm rounds and decoratively carved, parboiled and refreshed
Ponzu sauce (p.31)

Prepare and serve this dish as for shabu-shabu, keeping in mind the delicate flesh of the fish and the care required in cooking to retain its succulence. Serve with accompanying condiments and spicy sauces.
Serves 6

Kaki dote-nabe *(River bank oyster stew)*

This is another one-pot dish cooked at the table. The inside rim of the casserole is thickly coated with miso to resemble the banks of a river. The miso gradually makes its way into the well flavoured simmering stew.

1 kg large oysters (removed from shell or bottled)
1 tablespoon salt
3 shallots or leeks, cut diagonally into 4 cm lengths
3 bunches edible chrysanthemum leaves, broken into sprigs
500 g whole enokitake or button mushrooms, trimmed
6 fresh shiitake mushrooms or open cap mushrooms, wiped and trimmed with decoratively notched

crosses in the top of each cap
¼ head Japanese cabbage, cut crosswise into 4 cm lengths
6 tablespoons red miso
6 tablespoons white miso
1 tablespoon mirin wine
½ cup cold dashi
8 × 13 cm pieces giant kelp (konbu), scored several times to release flavour
1 litre dashi (stock)
6 eggs (optional)

Using the back of a spoon, mix together the two types of miso. Add one tablespoon mirin and ½ cup cold dashi to soften the miso and combine well. With a pliable spatula spread the paste over the upper inside of a 23 cm earthenware casserole or skillet in a very smooth layer about ¾ cm thick.

Bring the dish to the heating unit at the table. Place the kelp in the casserole then add one litre of cool dashi. Bring to boil then reduce heat to a gentle simmer. The guests then dip the various foods into the bubbling stock as desired. Each diner should scrape a little miso into the stock as required.

The oysters will only need seconds in the stock to heat through. No sauce accompanies this dish but cooked morsels can be dipped in beaten egg before being eaten. A raw egg may be placed in a dipping sauce dish at each guest's setting.
Serves 6

Yakimono and Teppan-yaki
Grilled and Pan-fried Foods

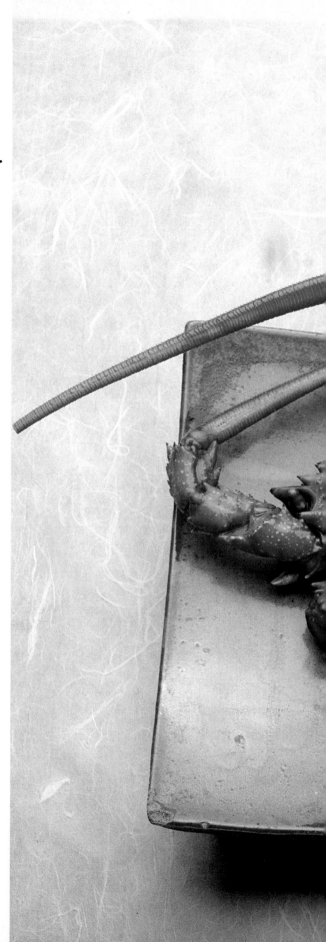

Yakimono literally means 'grilled things' but also includes pan-fried and oven-baked dishes. The aim of this method of cooking is to achieve a crisp, flavoursome exterior and a moist, tender interior. As with most other categories of Japanese cooking, fish features prominently. Salt-grilled fish is a particularly tasty example of yakimono.

These recipes adapt very well to Australian-style barbecues and make a delicious and exotic change from the traditional steak and sausages. Meat for yakimono dishes only needs to be marinated briefly to tenderise and emphasise its natural flavour. Piquant dipping sauces are the best accompaniments.

Teppan-yaki or 'mixed grill' restaurants are popular throughout Japan. Patrons can choose their own cuts and watch the chef cook them on an iron griddle built into the centre of the dining table. All types of seafood, chicken, red meat and sliced vegetables are cooked teppan-yaki style.

Onigara-yaki (green lobster or prawns)

Tai takara-bune (snapper)

Tai takara-bune (Snapper)

This is a specialty dish in Japan and is popular for celebrations.

1 × 1 kg snapper
2 hard boiled egg yolks
1 tablespoon salt
¼ cup mirin wine
1 tablespoon grated daikon

Clean and scale whole snapper gently, then fillet, leaving bones, head, tail and fins intact. This filleting method is called sanmai-oroshi meaning 3 pieces — 2 fillets and the skeleton. Pass a long skewer through the tail and head of the fish so the back is arched or concave. Sprinkle the tail and fins with salt and place under a medium grill until the skeleton sets in the desired concave shape. (This may take up to 30 minutes.) Remove from grill and carefully withdraw the skewer, twisting it slightly to loosen from flesh.

Cut each fillet in half widthways and slice into sashimi style slices, keeping the pieces together in order of size. Sprinkle each piece with salt and brush over with the mirin wine. For an interesting variation, the mirin wine may be combined with a mashed sea urchin before it is brushed onto the fish pieces to add an unusual flavour to the dish. Grate the egg yolks or pass them through a strainer. Place the fish under a moderate grill for 15 minutes, remove and sprinkle with the grated yolks and return to grill for a further 2 minutes. Remove fish carefully from grill.

Place the fish skeleton onto a serving platter and place a folded sheet of rice paper on it. Arrange the fish pieces neatly over it and serve with the grated daikon and soy sauce.
Serves 3–4

Gyuniku teriyaki (Steak teriyaki)

Teri means 'glossy lustre'. The success of this dish depends on reducing the sauce without overcooking the meat.

4 × 225 g sirloin steaks, about 2.5 cm thick
salt
2 tablespoons vegetable oil
4 tablespoons saké
3 tablespoons mirin wine
2 tablespoons dark soy sauce
mustard paste (see Glossary of Ingredients)

Salt steaks lightly on both sides to extract juices. Heat a little oil in a large, shallow pan and brown on one side, covered, over a high heat for about 3 minutes. Turn once only and brown other side. While meat is frying on the second side, splash on the saké. Cover and fry a further 2 minutes. This browning will produce a considerable amount of smoke which is why it is best done covered. Remove steaks to a side plate.

Over the heat add mirin and dark soy to the meat juices. As soon as the meat glaze is dissolved return steaks to the pan to coat with the sauce, only about 20 seconds on each side. To serve, cut the steaks across the grain of the meat into 1.5 cm slices. This allows the meat to be eaten easily with chopsticks. Arrange on individual serving dishes and glaze with a little of the teriyaki sauce. Garnish with a dollop of prepared mustard.
Serves 4

Onigara-yaki *(Green lobster or prawns)*

1 whole green lobster *or* 5
   large green tiger prawns
3 tablespoons mirin wine
½ teaspoon salt
1 lemon, sliced
1 teaspoon Japanese dried
   basil
2 egg yolks
1 tablespoon soy sauce

Cut lobster tail in half. If using prawns, shell the body, leaving head and tail on. Pass a skewer through the tail to the head to straighten the prawn. Combine soy sauce, mirin wine and egg yolk and brush over the lobster flesh and tail. If prawns are used, brush the prawn flesh with the sauce.

Place the lobster or prawns under a grill on medium heat for 15–20 minutes. After grilling, squeeze some lemon juice over the flesh. Arrange the seafood on a platter and serve with chopped basil or sansho. Sprinkle with sliced dried seaweed if desired.
Serves 2

Masu *(Rainbow trout)*

4 fresh rainbow trout
2 pinches salt
1 piece green ginger
1 piece fresh horseradish
soy sauce
1 lemon

Clean, scale and gut trout. Carefully remove the backbone, leaving the head and tail intact. Thread a skewer through the trout and shape into an 'S'. Rub salt onto the skin of the fish and place under

a grill at medium heat for 15 minutes.

Remove from grill and withdraw the skewers. Arrange the fish on a plate and serve with grated green ginger,

grated horseradish, soy sauce and lemon pieces.
Serves 4
Note: As a serving variation, long stemmed pickled ginger may be substituted for the root ginger.

Masu (rainbow trout)

Sayori no-shio-yaki *(Garfish)*

5 medium-sized garfish
¼ cup salt
3 tablespoons mirin wine

Clean, scale and gut the garfish. Thread each fish onto bamboo skewers to form an 'S' shape. Sprinkle with the mirin and then with the salt. Place under a moderate grill for 15–20 minutes.

Remove from griller and withdraw skewers. Arrange the fish on a plate and serve with grated daikon or green ginger and soy sauce.
Serves 5

Sayori no shio-yaki (garfish)

Tori no yuan-yaki *(Yuan-style grilled chicken)*

2 small whole chicken legs
(thigh and drumstick)

Marinade (500 g chicken)
½ cup saké
½ cup mirin wine
½ cup dark soy sauce
3 × 7.5 cm slices yuzu
citron rind or lemon rind
(optional)
2 shallots or leeks
ground sansho (optional)

Bone chicken leg. Pull out tendons if necessary. Spread meat out flat and pierce the skin a few times with a skewer.

Combine saké, mirin and soy sauce and add yuzu rind. Marinate meat in this mixture for 30 minutes. Do not use salt; marinade provides sufficient seasoning for chicken.

Skewer each piece of meat with about 3 or 4 long stainless steel or bamboo skewers.

Grill, skin side first, over a high heat for about 7 minutes, or till skin is golden brown. Turn and grill other side for about 3 minutes. Avoid turning chicken more than once and do not overcook — chicken meat should remain tender and succulent.

When done, rotate skewers to loosen them from meat and slide out. Cut chicken crosswise into 1.5 cm slices and arrange portions of 6 slices or so, skin side up, on individual plates. Garnish with 4 cm lengths of shallot, marinated and grilled. Sprinkle with a little sansho powder if yuzu or lemon rind is not added to marinade. Serve either hot or at room temperature.
Serves 4
Note: No lemon or dipping sauce is necessary with this dish because chicken is seasoned by the marinade. The chicken can also be cooked on a barbecue.

Tori no teriyaki *(Chicken teriyaki)*

2 chicken legs (thigh and
drumstick), boned
vegetable oil
½ cup teriyaki sauce
(following recipe)
ground sansho pepper
(optional)
4 sprays coriander leaves

Pierce skin of chicken with a skewer to allow sauce to penetrate freely and to avoid shrinkage during frying. Over a high heat, add a small amount of oil to a large shallow pan. Lay chicken, skin side down, in the pan. Fry over medium heat till skin is well browned. Move the chicken in the pan from time to time to prevent it sticking. When browned, turn and fry, covered, for about 8 minutes. Remove from pan.

Over medium heat, add the teriyaki sauce to pan juices. Bring liquid to boil, stirring. After a minute the liquid will thicken slightly and take on a sheen. Return chicken to pan. Continue cooking, over high heat, turning chicken several times so that it is well coated in sauce. Remove from heat when teriyaki sauce has almost completely reduced — a few minutes will be all that is necessary.

Place chicken skin side up on a cutting board and cut crosswise into 1.5 cm slices. Place 8 slices, skin side up, in a fanlike arrangement on each individual plate. Sprinkle on a little sansho pepper and garnish each serving with a fresh coriander spray. Serve hot.
Serves 4

Teriyaki sauce

7 tablespoons saké
7 tablespoons mirin wine
7 tablespoons dark soy
   sauce
1 tablespoon sugar

Combine ingredients in a saucepan and bring to boil over medium heat; boil until sugar has dissolved. Use immediately, or cool and store in refrigerator.
Yields 1⅓ cups

Note: In some recipes, like steak teriyaki, the teriyaki sauce is quickly made in the pan after pan-frying the meat.

Robata-yaki *(Combination teppan-yaki charcoal grill)*

Robata-yaki is a combination of teppan-yaki ingredients cooked over a Japanese barbecue called a hibachi or a charcoal grill. Fish (both fresh and dried), meat, chicken, vegetables and even noodles can be used.

Robata-yaki cooking is very popular in America and Japan. It is bound to become just as popular in Australia where we are fortunate in having such an enormous variety of good quality fish, seafood, meat and vegetables available to us.

The method is almost the same as for teppan-yaki but hibachi charcoal is used.

Robata-yaki is prepared, cooked and presented in front of the guests, and the food is served using long handled paddles. Only a skilled chef can present robata-yaki beautifully from the beginning of preparation to the serving stage. The method of serving this dish is unique — the chef serves the food to his guests from a distance using the long paddles.

Yakitori *(Skewered chicken)*

350 g chicken livers, cut in
   half, rinsed and drained
1 kg chicken meat, boned
   and cut in 2.5 cm pieces
4 red capsicums, seeded
   and cut into 2.5 cm
   squares
8 leeks, cut crosswise into
   2.5 cm lengths
Yakitori sauce (following
   recipe)
ground sansho pepper
seven-spice mixture
bamboo skewers, soaked in
   water for twenty minutes
   prior to use

Thread prepared livers, chicken, capsicum and leeks onto skewers. Grill over a high heat or coals, turning occasionally until the juices begin to flow out of the foods.

Brush with yakitori sauce or dip kebabs into the sauce and continue grilling, allowing excess sauce to drip back into a pot so coals do not flare up. Do not overcook or food will be dry.

Remove to a serving platter. Allow guests to sprinkle on some fragrant sansho pepper powder or seven-spice mixture before eating.
Serves 4
Note: Vegetables and chicken livers can be omitted or other vegetables substituted.

Yakitori sauce

6 tablespoons saké
¾ cup dark soy sauce
3 tablespoons mirin wine
2 tablespoons sugar

Combine ingredients in a saucepan and bring to the boil to burn off alcohol.
Yields 2 cups

Yakitori (skewered chicken)

Buri teriyaki *(Yellowtail teriyaki)*

For fish teriyaki, buy fatty fish such as yellowtail, mackerel or fresh tuna. The flavours of these fish lend themselves particularly well to this method of preparation. Either fillets or steaks can be used. A technique to use with oily fish is to douse it with boiling water after frying. This lightens the texture and flavour; the teriyaki sauce adds strength. Place cooked fish fillets or steaks in a small flat sieve or strainer tray — they are easily broken and damaged in a deep, rounded colander.

1 kg yellowtail fillets (with skin), cut crosswise into 4 pieces of equal size
salt
4 sprays coriander leaves
4 pickled ginger shoots *or* crisp cucumber strips
½ cup teriyaki sauce (p.55)
vegetable oil

Sprinkle fish with salt. Heat a small amount of oil in a heavy based pan, place over a high heat and gently add fish pieces, skin side down. Move fish carefully while cooking to prevent it sticking. Turn with a fish slice only once. When fish is half done remove from pan, pour boiling water over it to remove excess oil and return to pan. Add teriyaki sauce. Heat till sauce begins to bubble. Tilt pan and turn fish slices to evenly coat with the sauce. Remove fish to serving plates and keep warm.

Reduce sauce left in pan to deglaze and provide a good sheen. Spoon sauce over the fish. Garnish each plate with a coriander spray and a ginger shoot or the garnish of your choice.
Serves 4

Horaku-yaki *(Seafood platter on a bed of pine needles)*

2 fillets white fleshed fish, sprinkled with salt and cut into 4 pieces
8 whole king prawns, deveined but with heads and shells intact
8 fresh shiitake mushrooms (or large cap mushrooms), wiped and trimmed
pine needles, rinsed and wiped clean
4 candied chestnuts
24 ginkgo nuts in shells (optional)
rock salt or rounded pebbles
ponzu sauce
lemon slices or wedges

Gently grill fish, prawns, mushrooms and whole chestnuts. Roast unshelled ginkgo nuts in a dry pan. Roast rock salt in a dry pan and spread a 2 cm layer on the base of a casserole dish, or you can use river pebbles instead. Cover the salt with a thin layer of pine needles.

Over this arrange the fish pieces (skin side up), and then decoratively arrange the prawns, chestnuts, nuts and mushrooms. Sprinkle over more pine needles. Bring the casserole to the table and serve with ponzu sauce and lemon slices. A delightful pine aroma exudes from the dish.
Serves 4

Sakana *(Japanese mixed seafood grill)*

Sakana consists of a selection of seasonal fish and seafood e.g. garfish, jewfish cutlets, barramundi, salmon cutlets and snapper cutlets.

1 green lobster
5 green prawns
1 blue swimmer crab
5 yabbies
6 scallops or oysters
oil for brushing
salt and pepper
2 onions
5 Japanese mushrooms
2 tomatoes
2 capsicums
2 shallot stalks
2 bamboo shoots

Brush the raw seafood with oil, season with salt and pepper and set aside for 10 minutes. Slice the onion thickly, securing each slice with a toothpick. Soak the mushrooms in warm water for 5 minutes. Slice the tomatoes thickly and cut the capsicum into thick rings. Cut the shallot stalks into 7.5 cm lengths and the bamboo shoots into 5 cm lengths.

Cook the seafood on an iron barbecue at a high temperature for 5 minutes. Arrange the sliced vegetables on the grill with the seafood and cook for a further 10 minutes.

Serve with soy bean paste, sesame paste, sweet mustard paste, horseradish and soy sauce with garlic.
Serves 3
Note: Rainbow trout may be used for this dish but it must be wrapped in foil as the flesh is extremely delicate and may fall apart on heating. This method is similar to steam cooking. It retains the shape of the fish and makes the removal of bones easier.

58

Niku (mixed grill)

Niku (Japanese mixed grill)

**500 g eye fillet or scotch
  fillet
2 onions
5 Japanese mushrooms
2 tomatoes
2 capsicums
2 shallot stalks
2 bamboo shoots**

Cut the steak into 2.5 cm thick
slices. Make a shallow criss-
cross incision on one side of
each piece of steak. Rub with
oil, season with salt and pepper
and leave for 10 minutes. Cook
the meat over high heat for 2
minutes then arrange
vegetables on the grill and
cook for 10 minutes longer.
  Serve niku hot with soy

bean paste, sesame paste, sweet
mustard paste, horseradish,
and soy and garlic sauce.
Serves 2–3
Note: As a variation, the niku
ingredients may be marinated
in soy bean paste and saké for
2–3 hours before cooking.
Other vegetables may be
substituted for those in the
recipe.

Dengaku miso toppings

Dengaku refers to miso-topped grilled food. Both these delicious toppings are suitable for dengaku dishes.

White miso
200 g white miso
2 egg yolks
2 tablespoons saké
2 tablespoons mirin wine
2 tablespoons sugar
7 tablespoons dashi

Red miso
150 g red miso
3 tablespoons white miso
2 egg yolks
2 tablespoons saké
2 tablespoons mirin wine
2 tablespoons sugar
7 tablespoons dashi

Fragrant seasonings
(use only one)
ground toasted sesame
seeds
grated rind of yuzu citron,
lime or lemon
fresh ginger juice
ground kinome leaves (see
Glossary of Ingredients)

Place miso in top of a double saucepan and blend in egg yolks, saké, mirin and sugar. Place over gently simmering water and gradually add dashi. Stir until thick and well combined. At the last minute add one of the fragrant seasonings.

Always prepare dengaku miso in large quantities for ease of handling. Allow to cool to room temperature. Refrigerate and use as required. Both keep very well.

Kaibashira dengaku (Scallop dengaku)

This dish is a rather recent addition to the Japanese cuisine and combines native traditions with European technique and flavour.

700 g scallops, cleaned,
rinsed and dried
salt
vegetable oil
white and red dengaku miso
toppings
ground toasted sesame
seeds

Sprinkle scallops lightly with salt and place in individual oiled casserole dishes or shells.

Cover scallops with miso topping in a layer about half a centimetre thick. Bake in a hot oven for 3–4 minutes. Remove and sprinkle with ground

sesame seeds. Serve immediately.
Serves 4
Note: Be careful with timing: if overcooked the scallops will be tough and rubbery.

Nasu dengaku (Eggplant dengaku)

6 small eggplants
vegetable oil
white and red dengaku miso
toppings
fresh coriander

Wash and dry eggplants. Remove stems and cut in half lengthwise. Cross-score cut surface to prevent topping sliding off. Brush both skin and flesh with oil. Pierce each half eggplant crosswise with the skewers if you intend to grill them. They may also be pan-

fried in oil or even deep-fried. Cook until tender, turning as little as possible.

Apply topping to cut surface. If grilling you may grill the topping until golden. Serve immediately garnished with fresh coriander sprays.
Serves 4

Stocks and Soups

Dashi (Basic stock)

Dashi, an all-purpose seasoning and soup stock is a very important and highly valued Japanese cooking ingredient. It provides Japanese food with a unique, characteristic flavour and the success of a dish can hinge on the quality of the dashi. Making good dashi is the first principle of the wonderful art of Japanese cooking.

Today, most Japanese cooks use instant dashi as westerners use stock cubes — packaged granules that dissolve instantly in hot water. This is marketed as dashi-no-moto or 'stock essence'. Although it is tempting to resort to instant preparations it is important to understand the traditional method of preparing the highest quality dashi.

Nothing can compare in subtle flavour and delicate aroma with fresh dashi made from flaked, dried bonito. The bonito is dried in shade in the open air over months. It is sold in the form of sticks which look rather like pieces of wood. When purchasing bonito the denser the stick the better the quality. For maximum flavour it should be used as quickly as possible, however, it will keep quite well in an airtight container or in the refrigerator. Shave the flakes just before using for best results. The shaving is a time-consuming process but commercially prepared and packaged flakes called lana-katsuo are available.

Suimono and Shirumono (Soups)

Clear soup, known as suimono or 'something to drink' is served between courses to refresh and stimulate the palate as sorbet does in French cuisine. It can also be served with the final rice course in place of the more common thicker broths. Clear soup is always served in a covered lacquered bowl which, when opened, reveals an exquisite floating arrangement of vegetables and garnish.

Other ingredients are added to the well flavoured stock for balance and flavour — fish, chicken, egg, shellfish, sliced vegetables or tofu. All elements of the soup must balance and complement each other; for example shredded seaweed goes well with bamboo shoots, or paper-thin slices of mushroom with prawns. Garnishes such as pepper leaves, shreds of citrus peel or coriander sprays are also added for decoration and fragrance.

Another category of soups is shirumono or thick broths, made from stock and miso paste and so full of meat and vegetables they can be substantial meals in themselves. Miso soup is traditionally served at Japanese breakfast but also appears at other meals throughout the day.

Dashi with vegetable garnish, Nameko jiru (golden mushroom soy soup) and Miso-shiru (tofu miso soup)

Ichiban dashi *(Primary dashi)*

Freshly made primary dashi is best for clear soups which should be delicate enough to distinguish individual flavours and aromas. Leftover dashi can be frozen but a lot of the flavour and aroma are lost. It can be kept for a few days in the refrigerator.

1 litre cold water
30 g giant kelp (konbu)
30 g dried bonito flakes
(han-katsuo)

Pour water into a large saucepan and add kelp. Heat gently, uncovered, for 10 minutes. Kelp should be removed just before water comes to the boil — it emits a strong odour if boiled. To test if done, insert a skewer into the thickest part of the kelp — it should be soft and pliable. If it is still tough return to pan for a further few minutes.

Remove kelp and bring stock to a rolling boil. Add ¼ cup cold water to reduce the temperature quickly and add the bonito flakes. It is not necessary to stir. Bring water back to a full boil then remove from heat immediately. If the bonito is cooked for too long a bitter flavour will result. Allow flakes to settle for one minute. Strain through muslin, reserving the bonito flakes for secondary dashi.
Yields 6–8 cups

Niban dashi *(Secondary dashi)*

While the clear fragrance of primary dashi is essential for clear soups, secondary dashi has its place as a basic flavouring for thick soups and broths and many other dishes.

bonito flakes and giant kelp
reserved from primary
dashi
1½ litres cold water
15 g dried bonito flakes
(lana-katsuo)

Immerse the bonito flakes and kelp in the cold water and place over a high heat until water reaches boiling point. Reduce heat and gently simmer until stock is reduced by half. This reduction will take about 20 minutes.

Add fresh lana-katsuo and immediately remove from heat. Allow the flakes to settle then strain through fine muslin. Discard the flakes and kelp.
Yields 6–8 cups

Konbu dashi *(Kelp stock)*

Konbu (giant kelp) is a vital ingredient in Japanese cuisine. Good quality konbu has thick, wide leaves and a whitish powder encrusting the surface — this holds the flavour of the seaweed. Gently wipe this away with a damp cloth — washing will dissolve the flavour.

The flavour and nutrients of giant kelp easily pass into water, so it is not always essential to subject it to heat to produce a light, delicate stock. Simply soak overnight to obtain a deliciously delicate liquid. This liquid is often used in a primary dashi and is the basis of sardine stock.

Niboshi dashi *(Sardine stock)*

A delicately flavoured stock made from small dried sardines called niboshi; savoury sardine stock has a more pronounced flavour than bonito dashi and provides an excellent base for strong, rich miso based soups. It is often used in broth for udon noodle based dishes.

40 g small dried sardines
(niboshi)
1 litre cold water *or* cooled
kelp stock

To avoid a bitter flavour in the stock remove the heads and entrails of the sardines before use. Place the sardines in the water or cooled kelp stock and bring water to the boil over a high heat. Simmer gently for 7–8 minutes. Remove from heat and strain through muslin.
Yields 6–8 cups

Sansai *(Vegetable broth)*

Sansai is a combination of various vegetables served in clear stock. It is a very simple dish to prepare and has a distinctive flavour.

3 cups clear stock
selection of vegetables
(such as ginkgo nuts,
bracken, bamboo shoots
and mushrooms)

Arrange vegetables in 5 soup bowls and pour hot stock over them.

Serves 5

Ushio jiru *(Clear soup with snapper)*

5 small snapper fins
pinch salt
900 mL dashi
1 tablespoon soy sauce
1 shallot stalk, finely
    chopped
yuzu essence (if available)
    or 1 cm piece green
    ginger root, grated

Sprinkle the fins with salt and allow to stand for 15 minutes. Place fins on a plate and pour boiling water over them. Allow to stand in the hot water for 15 minutes.

Combine dashi with the soy sauce and bring to the boil. Place the fins into 5 bowls and pour the hot stock over. Place a few drops of yuzu essence or a little grated ginger in each bowl and sprinkle with chopped shallots.

Serves 6–8

Note: Tai soup can also be made using the flesh of the fish, filleted and treated the same way as the fins. Some accompaniments or garnishes for filleted tai soup are seaweed knots, prawns and ginkgo nuts.

Sansai (vegetable broth) and Ushio jiru (clear soup with snapper fins)

Tsumire *(Fish cakes)*

3 cups clear soup stock
6 sardines *or* 200 g fish or snapper paste
1 tablespoon chopped parsley
1 shallot stalk, curled *or* watercress sprigs

Combine fish paste with the parsley and form into balls the size of a walnut. Bring stock to the boil. Drop fish balls into hot stock. When they rise to the top they are cooked.

Remove balls and arrange in bowls. Pour hot stock over and garnish each bowl with a shallot curl or watercress sprig. Serves 4–5

Note: If fish paste is not available finely chop the flesh of white fish and mould into shape.

To make shallot curls cut diagonal strips from shallot stalk and place in ice cold water for 3 minutes.

Sayori soup *(Garfish soup)*

3 small garfish
1 shallot stalk, finely chopped
1 tablespoon soy sauce
pinch salt
8 mL dashi

Clean, scale and gut the garfish. Remove heads and tails and fillet each fish. Cut each fillet into 2 pieces and skin each piece, using the fingers. Cut each piece of fish lengthways once more to obtain 4 pieces from each fillet.

Take 2 pieces of fillet and knot together. When all the fish fillets have been knotted, place on a plate and pour boiling water over them. Heat the dashi, soy sauce and salt together.

Arrange the garfish knots in 5 bowls and pour the hot dashi over. Garnish with chopped shallot. Serves 4–5

Nameko jiru *(Golden mushroom soy soup)*

Nameko are slimy golden mushrooms which can only be purchased tinned in Australia. In Japan they are available fresh from the hills. Nameko are small mushrooms with an unusual flavour. They can be eaten raw or cooked.

100 g soy paste
1 teaspoon mirin wine
1½ cups dashi
100 g nameko (golden mushrooms)
250 g bean curd (tofu)
1 shallot stalk, chopped

Combine soy paste, mirin and dashi in a saucepan and heat gently to make a soy soup. Divide the nameko and the diced bean curd amongst 5 soup bowls.

Using a ladle, pour the hot soy soup over the nameko and bean curd. Sprinkle shallot over each bowl as a garnish. Serves 5

Ika-osui mono *(Clear cuttlefish soup)*

Ika soup is very popular in Japan.

1 piece dried kelp
2 cuttlefish
1 small piece green ginger root, finely grated
1 tablespoon soy sauce
pinch salt
½ tablespoon mirin wine
1 shallot stalk, chopped
3 cups clear stock
1 cooked carrot

Clean and skin the cuttlefish and cut into sushi style slices. Place the dried kelp over the cuttlefish slices. Cut the carrot into julienne pieces and place 1 stick of carrot on the kelp. Roll the cuttlefish, kelp and carrot up tightly and, using a sharp knife, cut into 2.5 cm pieces. Place the pieces into soup bowls.

Bring clear stock to the boil and add the salt, mirin and soy sauce. Finally squeeze the juice from the grated ginger into the hot stock. (Squeezing of ginger is called suppon-jiage.) Carefully, using a ladle, pour the hot stock over the cuttlefish in the bowls and garnish with chopped shallots. Serve immediately. Serves 4–6

Miso-shiru *(Tofu miso soup)*

Miso-shiru is often served for Japanese breakfast and dinner.

4 cups water
250 g tofu
100 g miso
½ cup dashi
1 tablespoon mirin wine
1 shallot stalk, chopped

Boil water with the dashi. Mix the miso and mirin together and add to boiling liquid. Heat on a medium temperature, being careful not to overheat (overheating causes loss of the miso flavour and bitterness).

Dice the tofu carefully into 1 cm cubes. Place the diced tofu into the hot stock and heat on medium for 5 minutes. Serve in small individual dishes sprinkled with chopped shallots.

Serves 4–5

Note: Kinugashi-tofu is the type of tofu most commonly used in Japanese soups.

Kai *('In the shell')*

Asari and shijimi are two types of shellfish used in Japan for kai soup. They belong to the same family as clams and pipis but their flavours differ slightly.

12 pipis or clams
1 cm piece green ginger root, grated
1 tablespoon soy sauce
pinch salt
1½ tablespoons mirin wine
3 cups clear stock
shallot curls for garnish

Soak pipis or clams in salted water overnight. Place a stainless steel utensil in with the seafood while it soaks as the metal helps draw out any sand from the shells. Rinse thoroughly and drain.

Drop the shellfish into boiling water and heat on a medium flame for 20 minutes. Add the stock, mirin, soy sauce, salt and ginger to the saucepan and heat on low for 10 minutes.

Remove shellfish from liquid and discard shells. Arrange flesh in bowls and pour the hot soup into each bowl. Garnish with curled shallots. Serve immediately.

Serves 4–5

Note: To make shallot curls cut diagonal strips from shallot stalks and place in ice cold water for 3 minutes.

Top: Ika-osui mono (clear cuttlefish soup), Tai (clear soup with snapper). Bottom: Kai ('in the shell'), Tsumire (fish cakes)

Mushi-mono and Tamago-yaki

Steamed Food and Egg Dishes

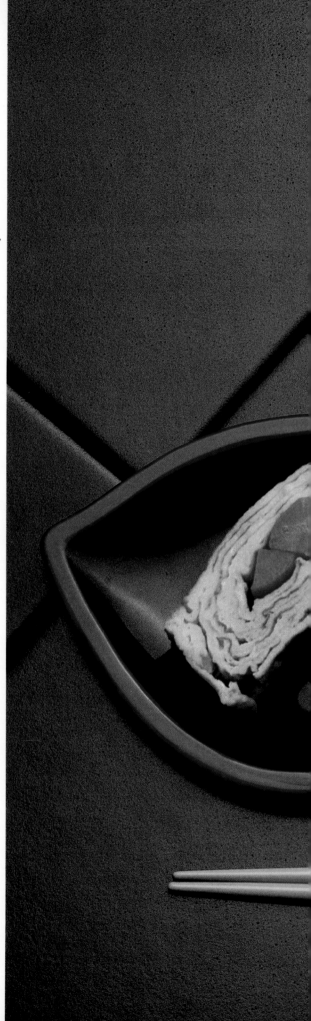

Steaming is a popular cooking method throughout Asia and indeed has many advantages. It preserves more flavour and nutrients than simmering and is particularly good for cooking very fresh food. Abalone and chicken are often steamed in Japan. Fresh chicken requires only 15–20 minutes cooking but abalone needs at least 2 hours to tenderise it.

The steamer should be very hot and steaming vigorously before food is placed in it — if it is not hot enough food will remain raw in the centre and will lose some of its colour and flavour. It is important to cook food as little as possible to gain maximum benefit from steaming.

Eggs are used in a number of different ways in Japanese cuisine, such as raw with one-pot dishes as a dipping sauce and steamed as savoury custards in small cups. Thick and thin omelettes are widely used as garnishes, as bases for sushi and rolled into decorative shapes to serve with vegetables.

Tamago-yaki (thick omelette)

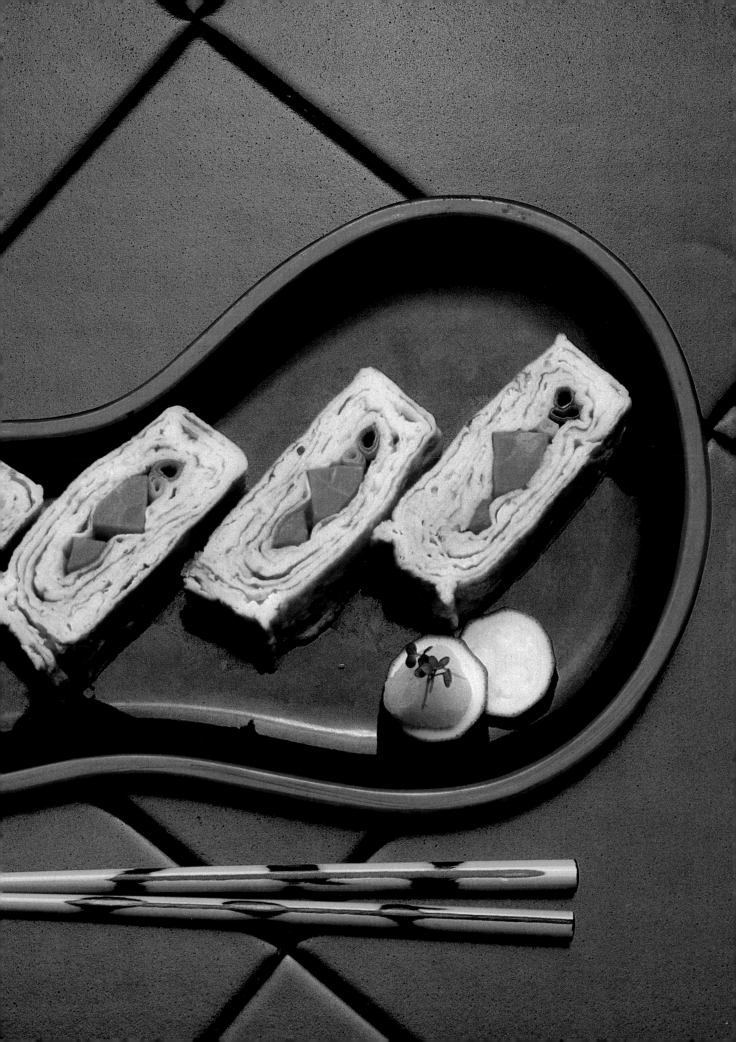

Saka-mushi *(Steamed abalone)*

8 cm fresh abalone in the
   shell
salt
4 tablespoons saké

Sauce
green intestine from
   abalone
1 tablespoon mayonnaise
1 teaspoon lemon or ginger
   sauce
1 tablespoon dashi
½ teaspoon dark soy sauce

While the abalone is in its shell, salt the exposed meat generously. With a stiff brush, rub the salt in — it acts as a cleaner. Rinse well under cold running water. Run a knife between the shell and the meat, but not deeply enough to separate them.

Pour saké generously over and between the meat and the shell. Steam, covered, for 2–3 hours over a moderate heat to tenderise the meat. Cool.

Cut the cooled abalone out of the shell. Trim off any dark fringed portions around the edge. Discard all of the intestinal tube with the exception of a piece 2½ cm long. Cut the abalone diagonally into 1 cm slices across the grain.

Rub the piece of intestine through a sieve. Blend with other sauce ingredients.

Use as an hors d'oeuvre or a first course. Serve at room temperature in small individual dishes with a small amount of sauce on the side. Garnish with seaweed.
Serves 3

Saka-mushi (steamed abalone)

Toriniku Shio-mushi *(Steamed chicken in seasoned broth)*

500 g chicken thighs
salt
6 tablespoons saké

Broth
½ cup broth (reserved from
   the steaming pan)
1 tablespoon dark soy sauce
2 tablespoons lemon juice

Score the flesh of the chicken fairly deeply to allow saké to penetrate and the meat to steam easily. Lay chicken skin side up in a pan, salt lightly and sprinkle on saké. Place the pan, uncovered, in a hot steamer and steam for 15–20 minutes on high heat.

Cut the steamed chicken into bite-sized pieces and arrange attractively on a serving plate. Discard bones.

Reserve the broth from the pan and strain. Add dark soy sauce and lemon juice to the broth, mix and adjust seasoning. Spoon over the chicken and serve immediately.
Serves 4

Variation
2 tablespoons sesame paste
   or toasted white sesame
   seeds, ground to a paste
2 tablespoons dashi *or*
   chicken stock
1 tablespoon dark soy sauce
¼ teaspoon sugar
pinch salt
1 teaspoon lemon juice,
   strained

Prepare and steam chicken exactly as above. Bring to room temperature and slice diagonally into ¾ cm thick slices. Arrange on individual serving plates. Mask with a few tablespoons sesame sauce and serve.

To make the sauce, combine the sesame paste or toasted ground sesame seeds with the dashi till smooth, then blend in other ingredients.

Usuyaki tamago *(Thin omelette)*

2 eggs
½ teaspoon salt
2 teaspoons sugar

Mix eggs lightly in a bowl without beating. Stir in sugar and salt. Strain mixture to remove strands of egg. Heat an 18–20 cm pan over medium heat. Grease very lightly with oil. Test pan for temperature by dropping a small amount of egg into the centre of the pan. If it sizzles immediately the pan is hot enough.

Pour a third of the egg mixture into the pan and tilt very quickly so the mixture spreads evenly over the base. Cook gently over a low heat until the surface of the omelette is almost dry, then using a spatula turn the omelette over. Cook only for a further few seconds. Remove from pan and allow to cool on a chopping board.

Degrease pan and use remaining mixture to make 2 more omelettes. Use them whole as wrappers for other foods or shredded into very thin strips for 'golden string' garnish.
Makes 3 × 20 cm omelettes

Nerimono *(Fish cakes)*

500 g fillet of snapper, cod
  or barramundi
1 carrot
1 thick shallot stalk
pinch salt
1 tablespoon cornflour
2 tablespoons mirin wine

Skin and bone the fillets of fish. Chop or mash them finely and marinate with the mirin, salt and cornflour for 3 minutes.

Spread fish mixture over a sheet of kitchen paper and form into a 12.5 cm square approximately 2.5 cm thick.

Peel and slice the carrot into 10 cm lengths. Blanch in boiling salted water for 2 minutes and drain. Place the carrot pieces and shallot onto the centre of the fish mixture.

Using the kitchen paper, roll the fish mixture tightly over the vegetables and twist the ends to form a bon-bon.

Place the bon-bon into a steamer and steam for 20 minutes. Remove from heat and unwrap.

Cut into 2.5 cm pieces and serve with green mustard (wasabi), soy sauce, basil seeds and mustard cress.
Serves 2–3

Nerimono (fish cakes)

Tamago-yaki *(Thick omelette)*

8 eggs
1 carrot
1 shallot
½ tablespoon sugar
½ tablespoon mirin wine
pinch salt
½ cup grated daikon
1 tablespoon soy sauce

Boil carrot and shallot till tender. Beat eggs with sugar, mirin and salt. Gently pour in a third of mixture to cover base of omelette pan. Place carrot and shallot in centre of omelette and roll across to other side of pan.

Pour a little oil into empty section of pan and pour in another third of mixture. Lift cooked omelette and let mixture slide underneath. From opposite side of pan, roll new mixture over cooked omelette, making a square

double omelette. Move to back of pan and repeat with final third of mixture making a square triple omelette.

Cut omelette into 2.5 cm strips and serve with grated daikon and soy sauce.
Serves 4

1. Beat egg with sugar, salt and mirin.

2. Pour in ⅓ of mixture to cover base of omelette pan.

3. Place carrot and shallot in centre.

4. Roll across to one side of pan.

5. Roll new mixture over cooked omelette.

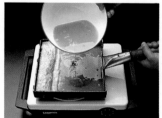

6. Pour in final ⅓ of mixture and repeat process.

Chawan-mushi *(Savoury cup custard)*

This is a delicate, stock-enriched, savoury egg custard containing prawn, chicken and assorted vegetables. Anything can be added that complements the taste of the custard base, including needle shreds of lemon rind, sliced mushrooms, sliced bamboo shoots or even udon noodles.

Special chawan-mushi cups are available wherever Japanese china is sold but you can use conventional heatproof dishes instead. Chawan-mushi can be eaten either with chopsticks or a spoon. Even though the custard sets completely the juices from the other ingredients give this dish an almost soupy consistency. It can be served piping hot or cold during the summer months.

80 g boned chicken breasts
1 teaspoon saké
1 teaspoon light soy sauce
4 small green prawns, shelled and deveined
1 lily root (yuri-ne) (optional)
12 stalks young spinach *or* watercress
16 raw ginkgo nuts, shelled and peeled
4 water chestnuts, sliced thinly

Custard
4 eggs
2½ cups dashi *or* light chicken stock
½ teaspoon salt
1 tablespoon mirin wine
1 tablespoon light soy sauce

Cut chicken into diagonal slices about 1.5 cm long. Marinate in the saké and soy sauce for about 15 minutes. Drain. Blanch prawns in hot water for 30 seconds, remove and pat dry.

Lily root is worth trying if available; its shape is similar to a flattened garlic bulb, but its flavour is mild and delicate. Separate bulb into segments and boil lightly for 4–5 minutes. Drain. Wash spinach or cress and chop coarsely. Shell and peel ginkgo nuts and use whole.

Beat eggs lightly. In another bowl combine the dashi, salt, mirin and light soy sauce. Pour stock gradually

into beaten egg. Mix well but do not aerate. Strain. Divide the solid ingredients except for the spinach between four cups.

Spoon the egg and stock mixture into the cups, filling them to about 1.5 cm from the top. Add chopped spinach or watercress. Cover each cup with foil, set in a steamer and steam gently for 20 minutes, or place in a water bath in the oven and cook at 220°C for 30 minutes.

Insert a fine skewer into the centre to test if done — it should come out clean. The custard should be just set but still jiggle freely.
Serves 4

Makunouchi

Dinner Boxes

A traditional makunouchi lunch or dinner box contains no less than 8 or 10 different foods. Rice moulds, grilled fish, sashimi, pickles, sweets, prawns and vegetables are just a few suggestions for a makunouchi dinner box from an almost endless range of combinations. Depending on what is seasonally available just about any cooked dishes that will travel easily can be included. Try a selection of the following:

cooked Japanese mushrooms	marrons glacés
oyster mushrooms	yaki-tofu
dressed up prawns	fish cakes
pickles	calamari sashimi
grilled sayori (garfish)	rolled beef
kobana-maki	makunouchi rice

Makunouchi rice is boiled, white glutinous rice formed into a cylindrical shape in special moulds. It is then cut into 3 cm lengths and sprinkled with sesame seeds.

A makunouchi dinner box is eaten on special occasions and is often prepared by a special caterer. The ingredients are presented in decorative lacquer boxes in combinations carefully arranged for artistic effect. Many years ago in Japan, people used to pack a makunouchi lunch and take it with them to eat whilst watching Sumo wrestling. These days lunch boxes can be bought at railway stations in the Japanese countryside, each area having its own particular specialties.

Makunouchi dinner box

Pickles

*T*raditionally, the most basic Japanese meal consists of rice and pickles. Such frugality is rarely found these days although some old people still consider this combination to be an adequate repast. In Buddhist monasteries where asceticism is a way of life, rice, pickles and a few vegetables are all that sustains life.

Pickles are much more to the Japanese than a condiment — they are a staple food of great importance. Once every Japanese family boasted a large pickle barrel from which the household supplies were taken daily. Commercially produced pickles are more popular today. Pickles are relished for their piquant flavours, their sharp, cleansing effect on the palate and their properties which aid digestion. Although many of them seem overpowering at first to the uninitiated westerner a taste for their unique flavours and aromas, which complement a Japanese meal so well, is soon acquired.

Taku-an (horseradish) and Nasu (eggplant) pickles

Yama-gobou *(Hilly root vegetables)*

5 yama-gobou (see
  Glossary)
1 cup soy sauce
1 tablespoon mirin wine
50 g chopped basil (yukari)

Wash, scrape and dry the yama-gobou. Combine the soy with the mirin and basil in a bowl. Place the vegetables into this pickling solution and marinate for one week. This pickling method for hilly root vegetables is called shoyu-zuke — pickling of vegetables with soy sauce.

After one week, cut the vegetables into 7.5 cm lengths and serve. Yama-gobou prepared in this way are most suitable for nori-maki.

Nasu *(Eggplant)*

5 × 7.5 cm long baby
  eggplants
200 g miso paste
2 tablespoons mirin wine
2 tablespoons grated ginger
¼ cup salt

Wash and dry eggplants and rub with the salt. Place eggplants onto a wire rack and allow moisture to escape from the skin.
  Combine the miso paste, mirin and grated ginger in a bowl. Place the salted eggplants into the bottom of a plastic container and pour the marinade over. Cover the container and allow the eggplants to pickle for one week before using. Serve whole or halved as an accompaniment to any meal.

Umeboshi *(Plum pickles)*

The Japanese call this type of pickling 'young pickles' because they are only marinated for one week. If more mature pickles are desired, the marinating period is extended to one month but extra salt and another 2 tablespoons of sugar must be added during the pickling process to prevent bacterial growth. If care is taken during preparation, the plum pickles may be kept for up to 6 months. During this time the plums shrivel and the flavour develops a great deal. The Japanese believe that pickled plums aid the digestion of food and provide fibre in the diet.

24 small unblemished
  plums
2 cups salt
5 violet-coloured basil
  leaves
500 mL saké
2 drops red food colouring

Scrub each plum with ¼ cup of the salt and soak overnight in cold water. Remove from water and drain.
  Combine saké with remaining 1¾ cups salt and place in a large container. Add basil leaves and food colouring and mix. Finally, add the plums. Seal the container and place a heavy weight on the lid. Store in a cool place for one week, stirring once during that time.

Taku-an *(Horseradish)*

1 giant white radish
  (daikon)
½ cup salt
500 g nuka (rice bran flour)
3 whole dried chillies
1 tablespoon turmeric
2 cups water

Cut stalks off end of daikon and rub the entire vegetable with salt. Combine nuka with water, turmeric and chillies and mix well. Add whole daikon to the mixture and place into a plastic container. Seal, place a brick on top of lid and allow to stand for one week before using to allow flavours to develop.
  It is essential to keep the pickle in a cool place to prevent spoilage. This method of pickling is called nuka-zuke. During the summertime taku-an may need to stand for only 3 days for flavours to develop.

Once the seal is broken it must be kept refrigerated but will keep for up to 3 months.
  Taku-an is served sliced with soy sauce. It is eaten as an afternoon snack or with the main meal or rice dishes. If daikon is unavailable turnip may be used instead.

Kyabetsu su-zuke *(Vinegar-pickled cabbage)*

¼ head cabbage
5 cups rice vinegar
2 tablespoons salt
4–5 tablespoons sugar
2 cups water
2.5 cm square yuzu citron
  or lemon rind

Core, rinse and dry the cabbage. Cut into 2.5 × 5 cm chunks. Pack pieces loosely in a preserving jar.
  In a saucepan combine the rice vinegar, salt, sugar and water. Bring to boil over high heat. Pour boiling liquid over the cabbage. Add the citrus peel. Cover immediately with a weighted lid. Remove to a cool, dark place and wait a couple of days before using.
  To serve, chop into fine shreds, place individual portions into small dishes and season with soy sauce. Keeps well, refrigerated, for up to two months.

A selection of Japanese pickles

Kabu no sokuseki-zuke (Quick turnip pickles)

It only takes an hour or so for this 'instant' salt pickle to ripen.
It keeps in the refrigerator for at least a week and is very good
with wafer-thin slices of cucumber.

12 turnips
5 rounded tablespoons salt
10 cm piece giant kelp
(konbu)
2.5 cm square yuzu citron
***or* lemon rind**

Cut off greens from turnips,
rinse and chop finely. Wash,
peel and finely shred turnips.
Place turnip strips and
chopped greens into a bowl
and sprinkle liberally with salt.
Press with hands to extract

water from the vegetable.
   Add the dry konbu and the
yuzu citron or lemon rind. Let
stand, covered, for one hour at
room temperature.
   To serve, remove small
portions from the bowl with

chopsticks and shake off excess
liquid. Arrange in a mound on
a pickle platter and season with
a little soy sauce before
serving.

Kyabetsu no nuka-zuke (Cabbage in dry rice bran)

This pickle is easy to make yet very tasty. Use any variety of
cabbage — green, red or Chinese — or giant white radish
(daikon); even turnips may be used.

1 head cabbage
1.75 kg coarse sea salt *or*
crushed rock salt
1.75 kg rice bran (nuka)
3 small dried red chillies,
seeded
10 cm square giant kelp
(konbu)

Core cabbage, wash and dry.
Cut head into eighths.
   Lay a piece of cabbage in
the base of a pickling pot.
Sprinkle on a layer of salt.
Cover with rice bran and
continue with layers of
cabbage, salt and rice bran.

Add the chillies and dried
konbu. Continue layering until
you have used all the cabbage,
making sure you end with a
layer of rice bran. Place a lid on
the pot and weight it down. Set
aside in a dark, cool place for
at least 30 days.

Remove quantity of pickle
required for use as you need it,
wash off adhering rice bran,
pat dry and slice into fine
needle shreds. Serve in
individual dishes with a few
drops of soy sauce for added
flavour.

Sunomono and Aemono

Foods in Vinegar or Dressing

These raw or lightly cooked foods served in vinegar or dressing are the Japanese equivalent of salads. Tiny portions may be served before a formal meal as an appetiser or at the end of a meal, before the rice.

Practically any vegetable, either raw or parboiled and a wide range of fish and shellfish are used for sunomono and aemono. Aemono dressings tend to be thicker and more heavily flavoured than the simple sunomono vinegar dressings. Ingredients should be cold and well dried before dressing is added.

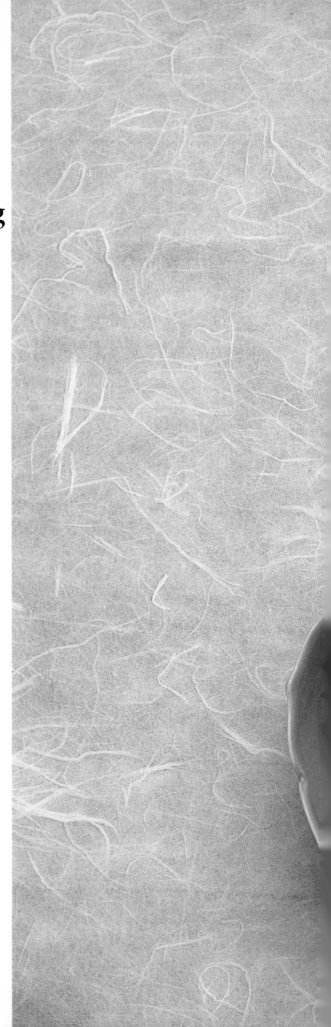

Mizoreae (golden mushrooms) and Nuta (seaweed)

Kisu-no-sunomono (Whiting)

The technique of combining kelp with the whiting flesh is called kobu-jime.

2 King George whiting
1 sheet dried kelp
3 tablespoons salt
¼ cup mirin wine
1 cup white vinegar

Clean and scale the whiting. Fillet, removing all bones. Soak the dried kelp in warm water for 15 minutes. Remove kelp and cut into 4 equal pieces. Place each fillet onto a piece of the kelp and press so it adheres. Sprinkle the salt over the fish fillets and allow to stand for 15 minutes.

Combine the mirin and vinegar with a cup of water and pour over the whiting fillets. Allow to marinate for 1 hour.

Remove the fillets from the marinade and slice thinly, sashimi style. Arrange slices on a plate, kelp side down, and garnish with a cucumber flower or cucumber peel spiral. Serves 2

Kani-no-sunomono (Crab)

2 large blue swimmer crabs, uncooked
1 cup vinegar
¼ cup sugar
1 small piece kelp
3 pieces lotus root
¾ cup water

Place the crabs in a large saucepan of cold water with one tablespoon salt and bring to the boil. Turn crabs over and cook on high heat for 20 minutes. Remove from hot water and plunge into icy cold water. Remove and drain.

Clean the crabs by removing the guts. Separate the crab legs from the body and place all parts of the crab in the mixture of vinegar, sugar, kelp and water and marinate for 30 minutes. Place the lotus root in a bowl of warm water and soak until it swells up.

Remove crabs from marinade and arrange on a plate to resemble a whole crab.

Garnish with the lotus root and serve.
Serves 2
Note: Queensland mud crabs may be substituted for blue swimmer crabs in this dish. Tasmanian snow crab is even more suitable. In Japan, the Japanese snow crab called taraba-gani is used.

Tako (Octopus)

Tako is another type of seafood which people other than the Japanese hesitate to eat, although it is gradually becoming more acceptable. Octopus prepared in a food press and roasted (called tako-yaki), is a much prized Japanese delicacy.

1 medium-sized local octopus
1 small cucumber
1 cup vinegar
¼ cup sugar
1 small piece dried kelp

Wash octopus and cook as for tako recipe in sashimi section. Plunge octopus into icy water to cool and drain.

Remove seeds from cucumber and slice into thin strips with the skin on. Combine cucumber with vinegar, sugar and kelp and use to marinate the octopus for one hour.

Remove octopus from marinade and thinly slice or chop into 2.5 cm pieces. Arrange on a plate and serve with wasabi or soy sauce. Serves 2–3

Sayori no-suzuke (Marinated garfish)

4 medium-sized fresh garfish
1 cup white vinegar
¼ cup sugar
2 tablespoons salt
1 small piece dried kelp (konbu)

Clean and fillet the garfish discarding the head, tail, fins and bones. Sprinkle salt over the fillets on the skin side and allow to stand for 15 minutes. Cut the kelp into 8 equal strips and attach to the underside of each fillet.

Mix vinegar and sugar together. Arrange each fillet (kelp side down) in a flat, shallow dish, pour the marinade over and allow to stand for 30 minutes. Carefully lift out each fillet and serve on a plate accompanied by wasabi (green mustard) and soy sauce.

Marinating foods in a sweet and sour sauce is called suzuke. Sayori no-suzuke (marinated garfish) can be used for nigiri zushi and sashimi as well.
Serves 4

Kurage *(Jellyfish)*

Jellyfish is readily available in Japan but in Australia it is more difficult to obtain. The Japanese variety is very different from Australian species.

Although the thought of eating jellyfish is distasteful to many Australians, it does have a distinct and quite acceptable texture and flavour when prepared Japanese style — it remains soft on the outside whilst the internal texture is quite crunchy.

200 g salted jellyfish
1 small cucumber
1 cup vinegar
¼ cup sugar
1 very small piece dried
  kelp

Wash jellyfish, place into a dish of cold water and soak for 30 minutes to remove excess salt. Remove and drain.

Wash the cucumber, cut in half and remove seeds, leaving skin on. Cut the cucumber into long thin strips and combine with the kelp, vinegar and sugar in a bowl.

Place jellyfish into this sauce and marinate for 1 hour.

Remove from marinade and arrange on a small plate sprinkled with thinly sliced seaweed. Soy sauce may be served as an accompaniment.
Serves 2

Nuta *(Seaweed)*

This dish goes well as a snack with saké.

200 g seaweed (wakame)
1 tablespoon toasted
  sesame seeds
½ cup miso paste
1 ½ tablespoons mirin wine
¼ cup sugar

¼ cup vinegar
2 shallots, chopped

Soak wakame in warm water for 10 minutes. Grind sesame seeds and mix with the hot miso paste, mirin, sugar, vinegar and chopped shallots. Remove seaweed from water and chop into 5 cm pieces. Add to the marinade and allow to stand for 3 minutes. Remove seaweed from marinade, arrange on a dish and garnish with a radish rose.

1. Soak wakame in water.

2. Mix ground sesame seeds with miso paste, mirin, sugar and shallots.

3. Add seaweed to mixture.

Hourenso *(Spinach)*

5 large spinach leaves
2 tablespoons soy sauce
1 tablespoon toasted
  sesame seeds
2 tablespoons dried flaked
  bonito

Blanch spinach leaves in boiling salted water for 2 minutes. Remove and drain. Chop into 7.5 cm widths and marinate in soy sauce and sesame seeds for 2 minutes. Remove from marinade and squeeze gently to remove excess liquid.

Arrange on a serving dish and sprinkle with the flaked bonito. Garnish with fine shreds of cucumber.
Serves 2–3

Mizoreae *(Golden mushrooms)*

200 g golden mushrooms
100 g grated daikon
3 tablespoons soy sauce
1 sheet dried seaweed

Combine the mushrooms and grated daikon gently with the soy sauce. Arrange on a serving plate and garnish with thinly sliced seaweed.

Mizoreae does not require any cooking and is served cold. It makes a refreshing breakfast or it can be served at lunch or dinner accompanied by steaming rice. The rice is good with soy sauce and raw egg stirred through it before serving.
Serves 2

84

Desserts

Japanese-style Fruit

In Japan fresh fruit is served as a dessert after the main meal of
the day. The Japanese are fussy eaters and expect their fruit to
be presented in an appealing way in order to bring their meal to
a satisfying conclusion. Preparation and presentation of fruit is
done with extreme care in order to preserve the beauty of each
individual piece.

    Sometimes fruit served for dessert is accompanied by sweet
beans (azuki), sweet bean ice-cream (ogura-ice), or plum wine
liqueur. The illustration of fruits demonstrates one of many ways
of presenting fruit Japanese style.

Sweets

Following a formal Japanese meal sweets are served with
powdered, whisked tea to complement its flavour. Made in the
shapes of fruit and flowers 'tea-sweets' are also served as part of
the ritual of the tea ceremony.

    Nowadays western-style cakes and confections are tending to
surpass traditional Japanese sweets in popularity, particularly in
the cities.

A selection of Japanese fruit

Daifuku *(Rice cakes with sweet red-beans)*

1 cup red-beans
½ cup sugar
2 tablespoons saké
pinch salt
1 cup sticky rice (mochi-gome)
¼ cup warm water
½ cup shinko (confectioners' flour)

Soak red-beans in cold water overnight. After soaking, drain beans and place in a saucepan of cold water. Bring to the boil and simmer for 3 hours or until tender. Add sugar, saké and salt and stir until dissolved.

Cook a further half hour. Remove from heat and cool. Using a mortar and pestle, grind the rice to a smooth paste. Add ¼ cup warm water and stir in the shinko to form a soft dough.

Turn dough out onto a lightly floured board and knead until smooth. Roll dough out paper-thin and cut into 10 cm squares.

Remove beans from the cool liquid and drain.

Place one soup spoon of beans into the centre of each square and bring the corners of the dough up and over the filling. Shape into a round and twist the corners. Turn the rounds upside down so the smooth side faces upwards.

Arrange the daifuku on a plate and serve with Japanese green tea as an afternoon tea treat.
Serves 4–6

Zenzai *(Sweet red-bean soup)*

200 g red-beans
200 g brown sugar
pinch salt
2 rice cakes (mochi)
1 sheet dried seaweed

Soak red-beans overnight in cold water. Drain and place in a saucepan of cold water. Bring to the boil and simmer for 3 hours or until very tender. Add sugar and salt and stir until well mixed and the sugar dissolved. Cook a further half hour.

Grill the rice cakes until slightly golden.

Divide the seaweed into 4. Wet fingers and form each piece of seaweed into a small bundle.

Cut rice cakes in half. Place one piece of rice cake and a bundle of seaweed in each of four bowls and pour the hot red-bean mixture over. Serve hot on its own or with pickled prunes or pickled baby eggplants.
Serves 4

Ohagi *(Rice and bean paste balls)*

The Japanese version of a European truffle, this confection is basically a glutinous rice centre surrounded by a layer of sweet red-bean paste. It takes its name from hagi, the willowy bush clover of autumn.

1 cup glutinous rice
1 cup short-grain rice
½ teaspoon salt
lightly salted water (to moisten hands)
2¾ cups puréed or chunky sweet red-bean paste
6 tablespoons kinako (roasted soybean flour) *mixed with*
4 tablespoons caster sugar
pinch salt

Combine two types of rice, rinse well and steam. When rice is cooked, remove from heat and rest, covered, for 10 minutes on a damp cloth. Sprinkle lightly with salt and mix in carefully. Then with a large wooden spatula mash the grains until the rice is half-crushed. While the rice is warm, form into balls by dampening your hands with a little salted water and patting it into shapes the size of a golf ball.

Cover with a thin outer layer of sweet red-bean paste about ½ cm thick.

Alternatively you can use the red-bean paste as a core, cover with a ¾ cm layer of hot rice and then roll in sweetened soybean flour.

Serve one to each guest with Japanese tea.
Makes 12 balls

Koshi-an *(Puréed sweet red-bean paste)*

180 g azuki beans
1½ cups sugar
pinch salt

Wash beans and cover with water in a large saucepan. Bring to boil and drain.

Add 5 cups water to pan with beans and bring to the boil. Reduce heat and simmer, covered, until beans are soft.

Pour bean water into a bowl. Place a sieve over the bowl, pour beans onto the sieve and rub through so that the pulp is strained into the water, leaving the skins behind.

Place the mixture into a muslin bag and squeeze out all moisture. What remains is unsweetened, puréed an. Place the an in a saucepan over a gentle heat and add the sugar. Stir with a wooden spoon in a back-and-forth motion — it will lose its sheen and lustre if stirred in a circular motion.

When the paste is thick, remove from heat, add salt and mix well.
Yields 2 cups

Zenzai (sweet red-bean soup)

Koshi-an made with sarashi-an

(Instant puréed sweet red-bean paste)

Sarashi-an is an instant red bean paste available in powdered form.

150 g sarashi-an
1½ cups water
1½ cups sugar
pinch salt

Place sarashi-an in a bowl, add a generous amount of boiling water and allow to stand for a few minutes.

When the solid an has settled to the bottom, carefully draw off the liquid. Add boiling water again, allow to rest and then pour into a muslin bag to squeeze out excess moisture.

Remove an from the bag and place in a saucepan with the sugar. Over a gentle heat, stir until mixture thickens slightly. Add a pinch of salt and mix well.

Yields about 4 cups

Mizu-yokan (Red-bean jelly)

A firm, yet very delicate sweet, this is always served well chilled. It is the lighter summer version of the heavy tea-sweet called yokan which is prepared from the same ingredients cooked very slowly until the mixture has the consistency of fudge. Other varieties include brown sugar, konbu kelp, persimmons and chestnuts. Yokan can be bought in cakes of different colours at Japanese provision stores.

1 stick agar-agar (kanten), soaked
2¼ cups cold water
sugar (optional)
700 g puréed sweet red-bean paste

Rinse the soaked agar-agar thoroughly and squeeze out excess moisture. Tear into tiny pieces and place in the measured water. Cook over a medium heat. Do not stir until the agar-agar is completely dissolved. Skim away excess foam and stir frequently until the liquid is reduced by 10–15%.

Strain liquid and return to pan.

Add bean paste and boil for 3 minutes, stirring constantly with a wire whisk. Remove from heat.

Place the hot mixture in a large bowl. Cool quickly and keep the bean purée evenly distributed and in solution by swirling over a bowl filled with ice cubes. Be careful as agar-agar sets quickly, at a much higher temperature than gelatine. When it has begun to thicken but is still pourable, place into a mould, a 23 cm square dish or cake tin or individual dessert dishes. Arrange green yokan squares and candied chestnuts in agar-agar.

Cover with plastic wrap and place inside a larger vessel filled with about 1½ cm of ice and water. Refrigerate.

To serve simply run a knife around the sides of the pan. Cut neatly into squares with a sharp knife so that each square contains a piece of yokan or a candied chestnut. Transfer 1–2 squares to individual chilled serving plates.
Serves 8

Note: Gelatine can be substituted for agar-agar but the result will not have the same texture or delicacy as an agar-agar based yokan.

1. **Dissolve agar-agar in hot water.**

2. **When melted, pour into tin.**

3. **Using chopsticks, drop green yokan and candied chestnuts into agar-agar and allow to set.**

Mizu-yokan (red-bean jelly)

Tsubushi-an *(Chunky sweet red-bean paste)*

180 g azuki beans
1 cup sugar
pinch salt

Cook beans as for koshi-an but for longer until beans are *very* soft. Return to heat, add sugar and stir gently over a low heat. The beans will be so soft that they will begin to disintegrate during stirring.,

The desired consistency is a thick, pulpy mixture in which the beans are only half-crushed. The bean paste should be softer than miso.

Yields 2 cups

Uji Gori *(Uji ice)*

Uji is a very small quaint river town just south of Kyoto particularly famous for its tea. The young leaves are ground to a fine powder and provide the high quality powdered tea (matcha) used for the tea ceremony. This green tea, mixed with a light syrup and poured over a dome of ice shavings, makes an elegant and simple dessert.

1 cup water
400 g sugar
1 tablespoon powdered
 green tea (matcha)
8 cups flaked ice

Combine the sugar and water in a pan and stir over a gentle heat until sugar has dissolved. Simmer gently until the syrup has reduced by about 25%. Cool and stir in the powdered tea.

Refrigerate green tea syrup, but stir before using. Place the flaked ice onto individual dessert plates, packing lightly to form a peak.

Spoon the green tea syrup over and serve immediately.
Serves 8
Note: Vanilla ice-cream can be used instead of shaved ice.

Awayuki *(Strawberry jelly)*

The word awayuki means 'snow drift'.

1 litre water
100 g packet agar-agar
4 egg whites
1 punnet strawberries
½ cup sugar
¼ cup plum wine *or*
 Cointreau
¼ cup milk

Break the agar-agar into pieces and place into one litre of hot water. Bring to the boil and heat on low temperature for 10 minutes. Add sugar and plum wine and stir until combined and the sugar dissolved. Pour the hot liquid through a strainer and reserve.

Beat egg whites in a bowl until stiff. Fold the egg whites and milk through the warm liquid and pour mixture into a rectangular, plastic mould.

Cut stems off strawberries and arrange in rows in the egg white and agar-agar mixture.

Place in refrigerator to set and cool.

When set, cut into squares and serve either on its own or with ice-cream or semi-whipped cream.
Serves 6

Awayuki (strawberry jelly)

Kuri-no-ama-ni *(Candied chestnuts)*

This is the Japanese version of marrons glacés. Cooking time is short, but the total preparation can take much longer. The addition of a little mirin or sherry makes an interesting variation.

500 g raw chestnuts, shelled and peeled

Syrup
300 g crystallised sugar
2 cups water
2–3 dried gardenia pods *or*
  1 drop yellow food colouring

Cut the base of each peeled chestnut off and trim body into an attractive shape. Soak chestnuts in cold water for at least 30 minutes to remove bitterness.

Make the syrup by combining the sugar and water and bringing slowly to the boil over a medium heat. Boil until the syrup is reduced by about 10%. Cool.

Drop the raw chestnuts into water with the cracked gardenia pods or yellow food colouring and bring to the boil over a high heat. Reduce to a gentle simmer and cook for a further 20 minutes or until tender. Cool nuts under cold running water and drain. Discard pod.

Return chestnuts to a pan and pour over the syrup. Cover and simmer gently for 1 hour. Allow to cool overnight. Serve at room temperature. Serve 2–3 each on individual serving plates accompanied by mizu-yokan or fresh fruit.
Serves 8

Kuri-no-ama-ni (candied chestnuts) and yokan squares

Mitsumame *(Cold fruit dessert)*

This is a year-round favourite, but is particularly refreshing in the hotter months. It consists of small cubes of agar-agar jelly topped with colourful fresh fruits, a tangy chilled syrup and a succulent little red bean called saru-endo or monkey peas. The beans are available canned, but can be omitted if unobtainable.

1 stick agar-agar
2¼ cups water
2 tablespoons sugar

Syrup
1 cup sugar
2 cups water
3 mandarins, in segments
3 peaches, sliced
lemon juice
¼–½ cup juice from canned fruit
small can saru-endo (monkey peas)

Tear the agar-agar into pieces and soak in water for several hours. Wash thoroughly and squeeze out excess water. Place in a large pan with 2¼ cups water and cook over a gentle heat. Do not stir until all the agar-agar has dissolved, then stir frequently until liquid is reduced by 10 per cent. Add two tablespoons sugar and dissolve.

Remove from heat, strain and pour into a 20 cm square baking pan lined with foil.

Refrigerate, covered, overnight.

To make the syrup stir the water and sugar together in a saucepan over medium heat till liquid boils and the sugar is dissolved. Remove from heat, cool then chill.

Peel and slice the fruit. Sprinkle on a little lemon juice to prevent discoloration. Cut the jelly into 1.5 cm cubes, using a very sharp knife for a clean cut. Then run a knife between the pan and the jelly,

lift out the foil lining and transfer equal portions of cubes to individual serving dishes.

Top jelly squares with the sliced fruit and syrup and 1 tablespoon monkey peas if available. It may also be served in a large glass bowl topped with any array of colourful fruits. With a scoop of ice-cream on the side this dish is called cream mitsumame. You may also add a liqueur of your choice to the syrup.
Serves 6

Glossary of Ingredients

AGAR-AGAR (kanten) A sparkling, pure form of gelatine processed from a type of red seaweed called tengusa, or 'heavenly grass'. In Japanese cooking, agar-agar is generally used for sweets and confections. One of its valuable properties is that it sets without refrigeration, at 42°C to 39°C (108° to 102°F) sealing in the freshness of fruits and other foods.

AZUKI BEANS (red beans) These small red beans are the most frequently used legume in Japanese cooking besides soy beans. They are steamed with glutinous rice for special occasions, or more commonly, boiled with sugar to make sweet red bean paste which forms the basis of a large percentage of Japanese sweets and confections.

BAMBOO SHOOTS (takenoko) One of the most common ingredients in Asian cooking; their relatively mild taste blends perfectly with other ingredients, picking up the flavour of the soup or stew they are added to while retaining their distinctive crunchy texture. Canned and packed in water or packaged fresh they are available from any Japanese provision store.

BEAN CURD (tofu) Made from soy beans and extremely high in protein while relatively low in cost, bean curd is soft and easily digestible. It is ideal for slimming, being very low in kilojoules. Bean curd is used fresh, usually on the day it is made; however vacuum packed varieties are quite acceptable. Toasted bean curd (yaki-tofu) has a stronger flavour and is popular for pot-cooking. It is fairly widely available in cans.

BONITO, DRIED (katsuo-bushi) The bonito, a member of the mackerel family, has been an integral part of the Japanese diet for many centuries. It can be bought steamed and flake-dried ready to be added to a dashi (stock) for instant flavour. Dried bonito thread-shavings are also readily available and usually used as a garnish to complete a soup. Fish stock is available in the form of dried granules as well.

BRACKEN (warabi) A fern widely used in pot cooking, steamed dishes and pickles; bracken can be bought dried or vacuum packed from Asian food stores.

CABBAGE, JAPANESE (hakusai) This large, leafy vegetable is pale green at the top of the crinkle-edged leaves and creamy-white at the stem where stalks are thick and tender. It is mild, almost sweet, with a more pronounced flavour than lettuce. In Japan it is simmered, used in pot-cooked dishes and in soups, pickles and salads.

CHESTNUTS (kuri) There are two main varieties —
tamba — large, firm and well textured
shiba — small, firm and sweet
Chestnuts can be bought fresh, canned or preserved in a thick syrup and are used in many Japanese sweet and savoury delicacies. They are also delicious barbecued.

CHRYSANTHEMUM LEAVES (edible) These are similar to but more strongly perfumed and fuller in flavour than the decorative garden varieties. When young and tender they can be eaten fresh but are more commonly parboiled, refreshed and served in light green salads. They are often incorporated into one-pot dishes to provide a subtle, yet distinctive flavour.

CLOUD EAR MUSHROOMS (kikurage) Often marketed simply as 'dried black fungus', these look more like chips of wrinkled bark or dried seaweed than mushrooms. The dried form must be reconstituted in tepid water for 20 minutes before use. They are added to numerous savoury dishes.

CUCUMBER (kyuri) Japanese cucumbers are smaller, have a much clearer flavour and are less watery than the larger varieties.

EGGS, QUAIL (uzura no tamago) Speckled brown eggs, 2.5 cm in length with a unique flavour and attractive size, these are used for garnishing soups and savouries.

ENOKITAKE MUSHROOMS These have slender, long, yellow stems topped by tiny round caps. Mild in flavour, they retain a certain crispness and aroma when cooked in soups and one-pot dishes. Fresh enokitake may be purchased from Asian provision stores and specialist greengrocers.

FISH PASTE (kamaboko) General name for a wide variety of puréed fish products. Kamaboko is sold in Japanese food stores; sliced, it may be added to noodle dishes, soups or slow-cooked dishes. Usually made into cakes or rolls it may also be eaten with no more preparation than slicing. Fish balls (tsumire) are a similar product.

FLOURS Wheat flour is not used a great deal in Japanese cooking, however it does have its place in noodles and deep-frying coatings. Rice flour and soybean flour are used more extensively in Japanese kitchens. Both are sweeter and contribute a nutty flavour to dishes.

GIANT WHITE RADISH (daikon) Daikon (meaning 'great root') is believed to aid digestion, especially of rich, oily foods, and is one of the most popular ingredients in Japanese cooking. Japanese daikon are big, fat and juicy, really good for mukimono (vegetable sculpture and garnishes).

GINGER (syou-ga) Fresh root ginger is now readily available from larger food outlets. Choose ginger that is firm and blemish free. Peel away skin from root and store in dry sherry in the refrigerator until ready for use. Available pickled, preserved or dried as well, this fiery, pungent root has an important place in the Japanese kitchen. The best quality ginger is very tender and flavoursome and only available seasonally once a year in Japan. Remember that, in Japanese cooking, if grated ginger is called for it must be grated very finely.

GINKGO NUTS (ginnan) These are the fruit borne by the mature female ginkgo tree. Several layers of the kernel must be removed before a smooth white nut is exposed. This is prized for its delicate flavour and attractive colour and included in many steamed, grilled and deep-fried dishes. Ginkgo nuts may be purchased fresh or canned at oriental provision stores.

GINSENG A Korean root vegetable with an unusual, spicy taste, ginseng is used to make tea and wine as well as in cooking. It is also valued for its medicinal properties.

GOURD SHAVINGS, DRIED (kampyo) Dried to a long ribbon-like form these have two primary uses as they are both edible and decorative. They are used to tie or secure fillings in dishes such as rolled sushi. Available in cellophane packs from Japanese provision stores they can be quickly reconstituted for immediate use.

KELP OR SEA TANGLE (konbu) One of the two basic ingredients for dashi, the stock on which so many Japanese dishes rely for their delicate, subtle flavour; the leaves are dried in the sun, cut, folded, and packaged. Never wash konbu, as its speckled surface is full of flavour and wiping with a damp cloth is the only preparation it needs. It may also be finely shredded and either deep-fried or sautéed as a vegetable. Another variety of konbu comes in dried sheet form and is used as an edible wrapper for many Japanese delicacies. Seaweed tea (konbu-chan) is now becoming popular as well.

KINOME Young leaves of the prickly ash, these are picked in the spring and used for their aromatic qualities and as a colourful

1. Azuki beans
2. Dried mushrooms (kikurage)
3. Kampyo (dried gourd shavings)
4. Black and white sesame seeds and rice
5. Soba (wheat noodles)
6. Dried mushrooms (shiitake)
7. Candied chestnuts
8. Somen (rice noodles)
9. Ponzu sauce
10. Mirin wine
11. Rice vinegar
12. Konyaku paste
13. Wasabi paste
14. Wasabi powder

garnish. Small sprigs of parsley or watercress may be substituted as a garnish but the flavours are different.

LOTUS ROOT (renkon) Raw, this root has more texture than flavour. The flesh is firm and crisp and excellent in vinegared dishes, thinly sliced as a tempura vegetable or slowly simmered. It makes an ideal garnish. It can sometimes be had fresh in Sydney but is generally available canned.

MATSUTAKE MUSHROOMS Scented with the fragrance of pine forests these are only very lightly cooked to retain their unique aroma. Matsutake are one of the most sought-after delicacies in Japan and are as highly prized as truffles are by the French. They may be found in selected Japanese stores, sawdust packed and generally imported from Japan. Matsutake are never dried and rarely canned.

MIRIN A heavily sweetened, amber-coloured rice wine used sparingly to enhance cooked dishes and in glazing sauces for grilled meats. Alcohol content is very low and it is generally only used for cooking. Mirin comes in bottles of all sizes and is readily available in this country. Aji-mirin, or seasoned mirin is also becoming popular.

MISO (fermented bean-paste) A complete protein package full of aroma and flavour, miso forms a staple in the Japanese diet. It is not surprising that its use is both wide and varied. It may be thinned and used in sauces and dressings or spread on grilled

foods and it forms the basis of the much acclaimed miso soup. Many varieties of colour and flavour are available. You need not worry about using it quickly. It will keep, refrigerated, for up to a year. Miso is delicious used as a sauce with Australian-style barbecued meat.

MOCHI (glutinous rice cakes) Heavy and substantial, these are made by pounding piping hot glutinous rice into mounds or cakes of various sizes. They can be purchased fresh, factory packed or vacuum packed in plastic. Served grilled and accompanied by a dipping sauce or a wrapping of toasted seaweed they are usually eaten on festive occasions.

MUSTARD (karashii) The dry, ground mustard used in Japan is very fiery and should be used sparingly. Made into a paste with a little water it is used in dipping sauces, pot dishes and salad dressings.

NAMEKO MUSHROOMS Even in Japan these mushrooms are more likely to be purchased bottled or canned as they have a very short life and preserve extremely well. Nameko are very similar to button mushrooms but have a slightly slippery outer coating. They are distinctively amber in colour with an earthy flavour and can be bought canned from any oriental provision store.

NORI SEAWEED Dark brown dried sheets of nori are bought packaged and are lightly toasted till crisp over a gas flame to

1. Agar-agar (kanten)
2. Toasted nori
3. Kelp (konbu)
4. Green seaweed for sashimi
5. Seaweed paper for sushi
6. Red seaweed
7. Shredded dried kelp
8. Wakame
9. Rolled kelp

refresh just before using. Nori is chiefly used to wrap various kinds of sushi but is also crumbled or finely shredded and used as a garnish in savoury dishes. Australian seaweed has great potential for commercial harvesting.

OIL (abura) Vegetable oils are the basic frying medium in Japanese cooking; animal fats are never used. Use a light, refined oil such as groundnut or rapeseed oil. Olive oil is never used because of its very dominating flavour. Sesame seed oil is also used but only for seasoning, never to cook with. Commercially prepared tempura oil is a mixture of vegetable and sesame oil which provides a harmonious balance and a nutty flavour.

ONIONS This family includes onions, leeks, shallots and chives, all of which are used the world over. They are stir-fried, steamed, stewed or simmered and are integral ingredients in all cuisines.

PEARS (nashi) Japanese pears are apple-like in shape and texture. Yellow to brown in colour they are available fresh or canned and are very good as a dessert.

PEPPERS, BELL (piiman) These are much thinner skinned and more delicate in flavour than their western counterparts; when shopping for peppers buy the smallest, thinnest variety available.

PEPPERS, HOT RED CHILLI (togarashi) These small red chillies come in both fresh and dried varieties. The seeds are dangerously hot and should be shaken from the pod before use. Wash your hands well after handling and do not touch your eyes. Used sparingly they provide a fiery contrasting note in some rather delicate dishes. Dried red chillies are called taka no-tsume or 'eagle's claw' by the Japanese because of their fierce sharp taste.

PERSIMMONS (kaki) Best when purchased fresh and firm, they are peeled before use and typically served as a dessert at a Japanese dinner. Iced kaki (sherbet) or dried kaki (hushi kaki) are good to serve at afternoon tea.

POTATOES (jaga-imo) Two main varieties are used in the Japanese diet, both of which are thin skinned and relatively small. Sweet potatoes are also used in small quantities.

PUMPKIN (kabo-cha) Flesh is bright yellow, has a rich flavour and is pleasantly smooth textured. It can be cut into bite-sized pieces and simmered, or deep fried as a tempura vegetable. It can also be sculpted into an elaborate centrepiece for a banquet or other festive occasion.

RICE BRAN (nuka) The basic pickling medium in Japan

SAKÉ (rice wine) Used as a beverage as well as a cooking ingredient, the high acid content in rice wine also acts as a food tenderiser. Saké suppresses saltiness, balances fish flavours and takes away strong odours. It is widely though sparingly used and readily available from liquor stores. Plum wine (ume-shu) is also widely available in Sydney and is very good in desserts.

SANSHO (pod of prickly ash) This greenish-brown ground spice is tangy but not fiery. It counteracts fatty flavours, particularly those of chicken and eel. Sansho powder is available in small boxes and has a shelf life of about a year.

SESAME SEEDS (goma) Both white and black sesame seeds are used in Japanese cooking in their whole and ground forms. They provide a nutty flavour which enhances many sweet and savoury delicacies.

SEVEN-SPICE MIXTURE (shichimi) A robust blend of seven dried and ground spices, this may be blended to suit individual tastes and is available in mild, medium and hot strengths. It is lightly sprinkled over udon noodles, added to soups and used widely to season many dishes.

SHIITAKE MUSHROOMS Dark brown with a smooth cap and light pinky beige meat, shiitake mushrooms are a staple in Japanese cooking. They are widely available dried here.

SOBA NOODLES (buckwheat noodles) Carried in Japanese food stores these are sometimes available fresh in vacuum-sealed plastic packs.

SOMEN NOODLES (fine wheat noodles) These have an almost threadlike thinness and are available in both dried and fresh forms.

SOY BEANS (daizu and edamame) May be eaten as a fresh vegetable or selected for drying; they are also used to make soy sauce, miso paste and tofu. A rich source of first class protein, they make an excellent substitute for meat in many dishes.

SOY SAUCE (shoyu) A pungent, brown salty sauce that is one of the primary seasonings of oriental cooking. Originally used to prevent foods from spoiling during the hotter months, its popularity spread rapidly and it is now widely used all over the world. Soy sauce is made from soy beans, wheat and salt. Many varieties are available varying in strength, flavour and colour.

SPINACH (hourenso) Japanese spinach has small leaves, a delicate flavour and a tender stem in comparison to the spinach sold here. Choose very young, tender spinach as a substitute.

STARCHES AND THICKENERS (kata-kuriko and kuzu) When necessary, a little arrowroot or potato or rice flour are used as thickening agents in Japanese cooking. Natural evaporation methods are also becoming increasingly popular.

TAMARI Used in oriental cooking and sold in health food stores, this is a thick, very dark liquid with a stronger flavour than soy sauce and a clear, fine soy aroma. It is sometimes described as unfermented or raw soy because of its shorter brewing period.

UDON NOODLES (wheat noodles) Come in a fairly wide variety of sizes and lengths in both dried and fresh forms.

UMEBOSHI (pickled plums) These are soaked in brine, packed in shiso leaves and left to mature in a salty bath. They have long been respected as an aid to digestion and keeping the intestinal tract clear. Purchased in bottled form, once opened and refrigerated they can be kept indefinitely.

VINEGAR (su) Rice vinegar is produced in a number of strengths. Lightness and sweetness are characteristics of a good rice vinegar.

WAKAME SEAWEED Bought in dried form, it must be softened in tepid water for 20 minutes before use. Wakame is widely used in soups. It is highly nutritious and low in kilojoules as well as being decorative in colour and form.

WASABI HORSERADISH The name 'wasabi' translates from the Japanese as "mountain hollyhock". Wasabi is sometimes compared to western horseradish, but the two are not related in any way. Wasabi is very fragrant and less sharp than horseradish. The edible part of the plant is the root. Outside Japan, fresh wasabi roots are almost impossible to find, but two alternative products are available — powdered and paste wasabi. It would be possible to grow wasabi in Australia in high altitude areas such as the Blue Mountains. Powdered wasabi comes in small round tins, just like powdered mustard and is diluted with a little water to form a firm paste. Paste wasabi comes ready to use in small tubes and must be refrigerated after opening.

WHEAT GLUTEN (fu) Commonly used in soups, noodle and one-pot dishes; dried wheat gluten must be softened for 10 minutes in tepid water before using. It is high in protein and very low in starch.

YAMA-GOBOU A root vegetable in between a radish and a carrot in taste, yama-gobou can be bought in packets.

YUZU CITRON The yuzu fragrance is unique and resembles no citrus fruit of the west. The yellow fruit, about the size of a tangerine, has a very short season. Lime or lemon can be substituted for yuzu.

Index